Praise for
Searching for Trust in the Global Economy

"Based on solid literature and insights from recent interviews with managers across four regions of the world, Jeanne and Tyree provide extremely useful information about the CORR standards for deciding to trust – competence, openness, respect, and rapport. The book is timely in that it offers managers practical tools and tips for building trust, which is the scarce currency of both business and human life in the contemporary world."

Zhi-Xue Zhang, Director, Institute of Social Science Survey, and Professor, Guanghua School of Management, Peking University

"This well-written and engaging book will appeal to managers and scholars who are interested in international management and cross-cultural business relationships. The core of the book is an insightful typology that sheds light on how people in four cultural clusters decide if they will trust a potential new business partner. Vivid examples and quotations illustrate differences in the four cultural clusters, and the book provides tangible suggestions for dealing with cultural differences."

Linn Van Dyne, Professor Emerita, The Eli Broad College of Business, Michigan State University

"This book lays out an insightful cultural framework that provides a practical approach to unpacking the complexity of building trust across cultures. As a scientist-practitioner specializing in survey methodology, I'm eager to apply this framework toward creating trust with employees across the globe such that they feel safe and empowered to share their much-needed voices."

Elizabeth McCune, Director of Employee Listening, Microsoft

"In a single volume, Jeanne Brett and Tyree Mitchell have provided the tools to significantly transform our understanding of the dynamics of trust and culture in a global economy. This book employs the latest analytic tools of 'tight' vs. 'loose' cultures to understand trust dynamics; employs valuable interviews and ethnographic data from multiple regions of the world to add rich and meaningful texture to its assessments; is eminently readable by both academics and practitioners; readily applies its analyses to draw implications for improving trust judgments and dynamics between international business partners."

Roy J. Lewicki, Irving Abramowitz Memorial Professor Emeritus, Ohio State University

"Brett and Mitchell provide an elegant way to think about cross-cultural differences in trust. They use the most powerful recent development in cross-cultural psychology – the idea of tight and loose cultures – to break the world down into four clusters, each of which uses different tactics for building trust. This model will provide an 'ah-ha' moment to managers who have worked abroad, and a useful guide for those just starting to do business abroad."

Raymond A. Friedman, Brownlee O. Currey Professor of Management, Vanderbilt University

"One of the most important global business skills is the ability to build trust with people from different cultures. *Searching for Trust in the Global Economy* is seminal reading for anyone working in a cross-cultural context, whether in-person or virtually. The book is a must-read for all culturally agile professionals."

Paula Caligiuri, Distinguished Professor, International Business at Northeastern University and author of *Build Your Cultural Agility*

SEARCHING FOR TRUST IN THE GLOBAL ECONOMY

Jeanne M. Brett and
Tyree D. Mitchell

UNIVERSITY OF TORONTO PRESS
Toronto Buffalo London

Rotman-UTP Publishing
An imprint of University of Toronto Press
Toronto Buffalo London
utorontopress.com
© Jeanne M. Brett and Tyree D. Mitchell

Library and Archives Canada Cataloguing in Publication

Title: Searching for trust in the global economy /
Jeanne M. Brett, Tyree D. Mitchell.
Names: Brett, Jeanne M., author. | Mitchell, Tyree D., author.
Description: Includes bibliographical references and index.
Identifiers: Canadiana (print) 2022014155X |
Canadiana (ebook) 20220141630 | ISBN 9781487527952 (cloth) |
ISBN 9781487527976 (EPUB) | ISBN 9781487527969 (PDF)
Subjects: LCSH: Trust – Economic aspects. |
LCSH: Trust – Cross-cultural studies. |
LCSH: Partnership. | LCSH: Success in business.
Classification: LCC HB72 .B74 2022 | DDC 650.1/3 – dc23

ISBN 978-1-4875-2795-2 (cloth)
ISBN 978-1-4875-2797-6 (EPUB)
ISBN 978-1-4875-2796-9 (PDF)

Printed in Canada

We wish to acknowledge the land on which the University of Toronto Press
operates. This land is the traditional territory of the Wendat, the Anishnaabeg, the
Haudenosaunee, the Métis, and the Mississaugas of the Credit First Nation.

University of Toronto Press acknowledges the financial support of the Government of
Canada and the Ontario Arts Council, an agency of the Government of Ontario, for its
publishing activities.

Funded by the   Financé par le
Government   gouvernement
of Canada   du Canada

Canada

ONTARIO ARTS COUNCIL
CONSEIL DES ARTS DE L'ONTARIO
an Ontario government agency
un organisme du gouvernement de l'Ontario

Contents

Introduction

- *It's not, I trust, I verify; it's I verify first, then I trust.* (133, Lebanon)[1]
- *Trust but verify; people are not on the watch for distrust, but don't ignore signs either.* (150, US)
- *It's not like testing I trust you, but testing if you can do it.* (103, China)
- *You have to know the person before you're able to say you trust them.* (140, Brazil)

Trust – people's willingness to make themselves vulnerable to others despite the potential for exploitation[2] – matters. Trust facilitates cooperation: when people trust each other they cooperate and share information; when they don't, they compete fiercely for resources.[3] Trust contributes to economic growth, not just because it fosters cooperation but also because people who trust others are more willing to take risks and have less need for resources to protect themselves from exploitation.[4] Trust promotes successful social interaction and economic transactions.

People around the world understand the importance of trust, but they do not all think about trust in exactly the same way,[5] and they know if they are living in a high- or a low-trust society.[6] What is less understood is how people go about deciding to trust. When we asked 82 managers from 33 different countries "How do you decide whether to trust a potential business partner?" their answers were noticeably different, as illustrated by our opening quotes. In talking with managers who were engaged in the risky process of developing new business relationships, we wanted to know what key actions they relied on when searching for information to make the trust decision and what standards they used to evaluate that information and decide to trust. We were curious whether managers around the world engaged in the same key actions and relied on the same standards. We wanted to know if there were systematic cultural differences in the process of deciding to trust and, if so, why. These questions led to the research that underlies this book.

To answer these questions, we interviewed managers from across four regions of the world – East Asia, the Middle East/South Asia, Latin America, and the West[7] – who were engaged in new business development. Our interviews revealed four key actions and four core standards that managers used when searching for and deciding to trust. The key actions are due diligence, brokering, goodwill building, and testing. The core standards are competence, openness, respect, and rapport (CORR). The interviews also revealed that use of these key search actions and CORR decision standards varied by geographical region.

To explain the systematic regional differences in the process of searching for and deciding to trust a potential new business partner, we propose a simple framework defined by cultural levels of trust and tightness-looseness – the strength of social norms and social sanctioning of deviations.[8] This trust by tightness-looseness cultural framework categorizes East Asia as high trust and culturally tight; the Middle East/South Asia as low trust and culturally tight; Latin America as low trust and culturally loose; and the West as high trust and culturally loose. The key to understanding why managers in different regions rely more on some search actions and standards than others lies in understanding how their cultures vary in levels of trust and tightness-looseness.

You can use this book and framework to expand your understanding of how and why culture affects decisions to trust. You can also use this book to navigate the challenge of deciding whether to trust a potential business partner whether that partner is in East Asia, the Middle East/South Asia, Latin America, or the West.

We published a scholarly article about our initial research in the *International Journal of Conflict Management*[9] and a practitioner article in *Harvard Business Review*.[10] Writing this book gives us the opportunity to share an in-depth analysis of our findings and to share new insights regarding what we learned about trust during periods of a global economic downturn (i.e., COVID-19). This world historical event revealed just how risky trust can be – and how important trust is to maintain the strength and growth of the world economy.

Overview of the Book

Searching for Trust is the culmination of our research into the question "How do people decide whether to trust each other?" We intentionally interviewed managers engaged in new business development because it is a context in which the decision to trust has significant economic and reputational consequences. Once parties enter into an agreement to do business together, each is dependent on the other to fulfill the agreement. We counted on the risk inherent in this situation to reveal the nature of the process of deciding to trust a potential new partner that managers followed.

We also intentionally interviewed managers from four regions of the world – East Asia, the Middle East/South Asia, Latin America, and the West – because the World Bank identifies these regions as the major areas of global economic activity[11] and because our research questions were about trust and economic development. Although these regions are vast geographically, people within these different regions share history and worldview. Our analysis of cultural data in chapter 2 reveals that people within these regions share a perspective on trust and tightness-looseness. Our interview data, presented in chapters 3 through 9, reveal that managers within these regions share an approach to deciding to trust a potential business partner.

We identified similarities and differences in the standards managers from these regions used to decide to trust and the key actions they engaged in when searching for information to make that decision. We describe these standards, which we refer to as CORR, as well as the key actions managers engaged in to search for information to make the trust decision (due diligence, brokering, goodwill building, and testing) in chapter 1. In chapter 2, we introduce the trust by tightness-looseness framework that we use throughout the rest of the book to interpret the cultural similarities and differences among regions in the standards and key actions managers used when deciding to trust. Chapters 3 to 6 each focus on one of the four regions where the managers we interviewed lived and worked. Each of these chapters provides an in-depth analysis of how and why managers in a particular region decide to trust a potential new business partner, as well as our advice as to how to manage the trust process effectively in that region. Chapter 7 takes a comparative approach, cataloging regional similarities and differences in the process of deciding to trust.

The most important similarity across the regions is how central in-person interaction is to the decision to trust. We gathered insights from our 82 interviewees prior to the COVID-19 pandemic, which massively disrupted normal social interaction across the globe. Therefore, we thought it imperative to revisit each region to understand if and how the process of deciding to trust had changed with the social distancing requirements and travel restrictions associated with this global health crisis. We reconnected with 21 of our prior interviewees to ask that very question. We also asked if they thought changes to their business development process necessitated by pandemic restrictions would continue in a post-pandemic world and, if so, in what ways. Chapters 8 and 9 provide an analysis of those 21 interviews. Chapter 8 highlights what changed in the process of deciding to trust because of restrictions due to the COVID-19 pandemic. Spoiler alert! Although the pandemic affected all regions, the response in different regions was both similar in some ways and quite different in others. Chapter 9 focuses on the future, and what changes in the process of deciding to trust managers thought were most likely to persist in a post-pandemic world. Chapter 10 offers practical tips and tools for how to apply insights into regional cultural differences in the process of deciding to trust. It suggests how to address the CORR standard that dominates the decision to trust in each region and how to provide information via the key actions that managers in different regions rely on. Finally, chapter 10 addresses how cultural knowledge helps identify what is cultural (versus intentionally disrespectful), and how to use cultural knowledge when deciding to trust.

The Trust Literature

Why do this research on how managers contemplating a new business relationship decide to trust when there is a massive amount of scholarly writing about trust in psychology, sociology, economics, and management? Books, articles, and videos by scholars from many different disciplines address theory and present data about the meaning of trust, its determinants, its consequences, and the processes by which people gain, lose, and regain trust.[12] Many studies take a comparative culture perspective and find cultural differences.[13] With the exception of the World Values Survey, most of these culture and trust studies compare data from just a few, usually two, nations.[14] To draw global conclusions from such studies, analysts need to integrate the findings of multiple studies, but that work is complicated because different studies use different methods and measures, collecting data from different types of samples and in different trust contexts.[15] Often the most analysts can reasonably conclude is that there are cultural differences, but all the methodological and sampling differences confound a straightforward explanation for why those differences exist, much less what is cultural about them. Doing comparative cultural research is challenging. Interpreting it to generate general and practical knowledge is even more challenging.

Respecting these challenges, we designed our study to avoid some of the limitations of prior comparative culture research. We chose a particular context, deciding to trust in a new business relationship, and a particular sample, managers who were responsible for developing new business relationships. We also recruited managers from many different national cultures, which we could group into regions by geography, economy, and, importantly, by culture. These research design choices allowed us to compare, contrast, and provide a cultural interpretation of managers' experiences in deciding to trust a new business partner.

Culture and Searching for Trust

Culture matters when people are searching for trust. Culture refers to the unique character of a group.[16] Individuals have personalities; groups have cultures. Culture is the unwritten rules, called *norms*, that govern social interaction in the group. Whereas the *problem* of trust (being vulnerable to others in social interaction) is the same regardless of culture, the *process* of trust (deciding whether to trust another person) may be different. One reason is that the starting point, the level of trust in the culture, varies dramatically in different cultures.[17] Another reason is that people in some cultures adhere more tightly to the norms that govern social interaction than people in other cultures.[18] We thought it was likely that there would be similarities and differences among regions in the process of deciding whether to trust a potential new business partner. We just did not know *what* those cultural similarities and differences would be. We set out to learn.

The People We Learned From

Over the course of our research, we succeeded in talking with younger and older managers (average age, 37, range 25–54 years old); men and women (28 percent female); and managers in industries as diverse as financial services, mining, oil and gas, food and agriculture, technology, health care, insurance, manufacturing, and real estate. Their job functions ranged from sales, marketing, business development, project management, supply chain management, procurement, and consulting to research and development.

Although the focus of our interviews was what managers do when deciding whether to trust a potential new business partner, many managers emphasized that trust is a two-way street. They told us that they were trying to enact the same behaviors that they were looking for in a potential partner. As one explained, *It's both ways at the end of the day, you need to trust the partner, and the partner needs to trust you* (143, Singapore).[19]

We wanted to hear from managers in all different regions of the world, but our own language restrictions meant that we had to conduct our interviews in English. Ultimately, we drew our sample from people enrolled in advanced management education courses conducted by the Kellogg School of Management, Northwestern University. These courses, whether open to the public for an executive education certificate or restricted to those qualifying for an Executive MBA degree, draw participants from all over the world. (Kellogg's global EMBA program has sites in Beijing, China; Toronto, Canada; Tel Aviv, Israel; Hong

Kong; Vallendar, Germany; Miami, Florida; and Evanston, Illinois.). The managers we interviewed participated in one of more than 20 different programs across a span of two years. Each interview was conducted independently and, to increase the diversity of information, we explicitly did not include "friends and colleagues" of interviewees in the sample. Exhibit I.1 breaks down the sample of interviewees by region and nationality; it also indicates those with whom we re-connected in the fall of 2020 during the COVID-19 pandemic.

EXHIBIT I.1. *Region and nationality of interviewees.*

Middle East/ South Asia		West		Latin America		East Asia	
ID	Nationality	ID	Nationality	ID	Nationality	ID	Nationality
101	Kuwait	105	Switzerland	109	Mexico	103	China
102	India	106	US	110	Brazil	104	Japan
112	Turkey	107	Poland	119	Nicaragua	111	Thailand
113	Palestine	108	US	124	Colombia	118	Japan
115	Palestine	122	US	125	Ecuador	129	Korea
117	Turkey	123	US	132	Panama	130	Korea
121	India	126	US	137	Mexico	134	Korea
131	Turkey	127	Germany	140	Brazil	143	Singapore
133	Lebanon	138	US	144	Bolivia	155	China
135	Turkey	139	US	145	Brazil	158	China
136	Saudi Arabia	141	Italy	147	Mexico	161	China
146	UAE	142	US	157	Brazil	165	Japan
151	Palestine	148	France/Spain	160	Colombia	166	China
169	India	150	US	168	Mexico	174	Hong Kong
177	India	152	Italy	170	Ecuador	176	China
178	India	159	Germany	173	Costa Rica	184	Singapore
180	India	162	Finland	179	Chile	185	Hong Kong
182	Jordan	163	Germany	181	Peru	186	Japan
195	Saudi Arabia	172	Italy	183	Uruguay	189	China
		191	US	187	Mexico	192	China
		193	US	190	Mexico	188	Indonesia

Note: Highlighted IDs and nationalities indicate re-interviews fall of 2020. UAE refers to the United Arab Emirates.

Trusting a Potential Business versus
Social Partner

Although our research focuses on deciding to trust a potential partner in a business relationship, there are several reasons to believe that deciding to trust a potential partner in a social relationship may not be so very different. In both contexts, the decision to trust risks that the partner will exploit the relationship. In both contexts, the decision to trust involves gathering information about the potential partner. In both contexts, the ultimate decision is personal, a feeling, an intuition. The cultural environment in which people learn to judge trustworthiness in everyday social interaction is the same cultural environment in which managers decide to trust potential business partners. For all these reasons, we suggest that the interactions managers engage in to decide to trust a potential business partner are not very different from what they and others in their cultures do when deciding to trust a new friend, neighbor, or co-worker. Although our advice is grounded in what we learned from interviewing managers who were searching for trust to develop new business, it is likely to be useful whether the new relationship is for economic, social, political, or other purposes.

What May Surprise You

We suspect that some of our findings may surprise you – in particular, the similarities and differences among geographical regions in how people decide to trust. The geographical regions are admittedly broad. However, as discussed earlier, nations within different regions share two very important elements of culture that are central to the trust decision: levels of trust and tightness-looseness. Although the problem of deciding to trust is the same, the standards people rely primarily on are different. As well, although people in all regions engage in the same key actions when searching for information to make the trust decision, their reliance on different actions varies.

The research in this book offers productive ways to think about and address cultural differences and build new relationships, which are critical for growing and managing the global economy.

CHAPTER 1

Searching for and Deciding to Trust – Key Actions and CORR Standards

Deciding to trust a potential partner requires searching for information and analyzing that information against one or more standards. We asked interviewees, "What do people do in order to decide whether to trust a potential new business partner?" Managers told us about the actions they engaged in:

- *You start to do some pre-check ... to see if any of your current business partners had the chance in the past to deal with the company or person ... and you try to get at least a couple of this kind of references.* (141, Italy)
- *If Mr. B introduces Mr. C to Mr. A, then Mr. A would trust Mr. C, because Mr. A trusts Mr. B, and Mr. A knows that if Mr. C performs very badly, then Mr. B will be very embarrassed and the relationship between Mr. A and Mr. B gets very weak.* (104, Japan)
- *See if person is forthcoming; ask a question you know the answer to.* (142, US)
- *It's a common thing. People go on like dinners. Maybe the meeting takes like one hour ... but then, let's go on a dinner. And at night they*

have a couple of drinks, they talk about stuff, life and everything. So they try to get to know each other's character, and so they probably decide there whether to trust that person or not. (131, Turkey)

These quotes illustrate different key actions managers undertook in searching for information about the potential partner to make the trust decision. They sought reputational information about the potential partner and company, *You start to do some pre-check* (141, Italy), which we label due diligence. They asked for introductions, *If Mr. B introduces Mr. C to Mr. A* (Japan, 104), which we label brokering. They met and asked questions about the potential joint project, *See if person is forthcoming; ask a question you know the answer to* (142, US), which we label testing. They met in informal social settings with the goal of getting to know each other, *People go on like dinners ... So they try to get to know each other's character* (131, Turkey), which we label goodwill building.

Trusting a new business partner is risky. Managers had to evaluate the information they were gathering. To understand how they were making those evaluations, we asked, "How do people decide to trust someone new?" They told us:

- *It's not like testing I trust you, but testing if you can do it.* (103, China)
- *Sometimes people tell the things they cannot do. It's a big mistake and you lose trust completely. If you are in the industry, you know what's realistic and what's not.* (186, Japan)
- *I think you build trust by sharing information. ... If it's only give, and there's no take, or if there's only a take from his side and no give, then it's not a fair dialog.* (127, Germany)
- *Everyone can be different ... because people are different usually and you have to respect the choices.* (115, Palestine) *... if you show that you respect their way of living, etc., can play a big role in smoothing the starting.* (102, India)

- *If you don't know him, find out if he has same values as you do.* (157, Brazil) *You have to know the person before you're able to say you trust them.* (140, Brazil)

These quotes illustrate the four core standards that managers were using to decide to trust: competence, *It's not like testing I trust you, but testing if you can do it* (103, China); openness, *I think you build trust by sharing information* (127, Germany); respect, *people are different usually and you have to respect the choices* (115, Palestine); and rapport, *find out if he has same values as you do* (157, Brazil). We refer to these as the CORR standards for deciding to trust.

To decide whether to trust a potential new partner, managers compared the information they gathered via one or more of the key actions to their preferred CORR standard of trust. This chapter describes the key actions and CORR standards managers used in deciding to trust. It opens with a brief overview of the methods we used to organize and integrate what we learned from interviews with 82 managers from 33 different countries. After describing the key actions managers used when searching for information to make the decision to trust, we discuss the CORR standards.

Making Sense of the Interviews

There are many different ways of doing social science research. To investigate our research questions (1) "How do managers decide to trust a potential new business partner?" and (2) "Are there cultural differences in the process of deciding to trust?" we followed general guidelines for using qualitative research methods in behavioral science research.[1] We collected data from a pre-identified group of people – in our case, managers who were involved in business development and who were located in one of four regions of the world identified by the

World Bank as major locations of economic growth.[2] To analyze our data, we organized the information in the interviews according to common themes that surfaced in multiple interviews and we refined the themes as we continued to interview until no new themes emerged.[3] Researchers following this general method often engage in waves of data collection and data analysis, and we did this, too. We began by interviewing 24 managers from across the four different regions of the world, analyzing what they told us into themes, refining our questions, interviewing 30 more managers, analyzing what they told us, refining our themes, and so on. In all, we engaged in three waves of data collection and analysis. By the third wave of analysis, although we were continuing to deepen our understanding of the themes we had identified as central to the process of deciding to trust, we were not identifying new themes, nor were we aggregating old themes. This was a signal to end data collection.

By the end of this first stage of data analysis, we had identified the themes that would become the key actions to search for information to use in deciding to trust and the CORR standards for making that decision. In the second stage of data analysis, we re-read all interviews to identify quotes that illustrated the themes. We ignored regional differences in the first two stages of data analysis. In the third stage of data analysis, we sorted quotes into the regional location of the interviewee who provided the quote. This third stage of analysis allowed us to see similarities and differences in the way managers were searching for and deciding to trust a potential business partner.

This chapter develops the two sets of themes identified in the first stage of data analysis: key actions managers took while searching for information to inform their trust decisions and the CORR standards (competence, openness, respect, rapport) managers used to decide to trust. Chapter 2 develops a cultural explanation for the similarities and differences in the way managers in different regions searched for and decided to trust a potential business partner.

Key Actions when Searching for Trust

The quotes that open this chapter describe four different key actions that managers engaged in while searching for information to make a decision to trust: due diligence, brokering, goodwill building, and testing.

Due diligence refers to a search for information about the potential partner and the company the partner represents. Due diligence was not limited to reviewing the financial status and legal history of the company. Managers we interviewed sought all kinds of information to help them make the trust decision. For the interviewee who said, *See if any of your current business partners had the chance in the past to deal with the company or person ... and you try to get at least a couple of this kind of references* (141, Italy), due diligence involved delving into the reputation of the potential partner and their company. Some managers started due diligence by checking their partner's internet and social media presence. Most, however, sought reputational information from people who had direct experience working with the individual and the company. Managers did seek information about the company's prior business; however, in responding to our questions about trust, managers emphasized the value of personal references.

Brokering refers to the actions of a third party that change the relationship between two or more other parties.[4] Brokering, as it was used to search for information to make a decision to trust, refers to a special kind of introduction: *If Mr. B introduces Mr. C to Mr. A, then Mr. A would trust Mr. C, because Mr. A trusts Mr. B, and Mr. A knows that if Mr. C performs very badly, then Mr. B will be very embarrassed and the relationship between Mr. A and Mr. B gets very weak* (104, Japan). This brokered introduction is special because it puts the broker's reputation on the line. If the broker recommends a potential partner to you, and that person turns out not to be trustworthy, you will lose confidence not only in the potential partner but also in the broker. This is what makes brokering distinct from an introduction that results from due diligence.

In brokering, the third-party brokers stake their own reputations for trustworthiness on the potential partners being trustworthy in their relationship with each other.

Goodwill building refers to engaging in social interaction to get to know the potential partner. It can range from a few minutes of small talk at the beginning of a meeting to extended social interaction in a non-business setting. The process is described well by the interviewee who said, *It's a common thing. People go on like dinners. Maybe the meeting takes like one hour, but then, let's go on a dinner. And at night they have a couple of drinks, they talk about stuff, life and everything. So, they try to get to know each other's character, and so they probably decide there whether to trust that person or not* (131, Turkey). Opportunities for goodwill building can range from invitations to share coffee or tea to lunches, dinners, golf, sporting events, and even invitations to family celebrations such as birthdays, anniversaries, and weddings.

Testing refers to getting the potential partner to act or react and thereby provide firsthand data to evaluate trust. *I go to my network and ask them about this person, as I go into discussion with this person either the input that I got from my network is going to be confirmed or it's going to be questioned. If it ends up questioned, I would say my cautious level will skyrocket* (113, Palestine). Testing could be asking a business-related question to which you already know the answer or asking for a reaction to information on the company you collected in due diligence. The purpose of testing is not to try to catch people out, but to confirm and develop information already available.

Although due diligence, brokering, goodwill building, and testing are distinct actions for searching information to use to decide to trust, they are not mutually exclusive actions.[5] Due diligence, for example, may turn up someone who can serve as a broker. Testing can occur in the context of goodwill building. Furthermore, seeking information to make the trust decision is a process. The order in which managers engaged in these actions varied. Although most started out in a due diligence phase, others identified a partner they thought they could work with and then engaged in due diligence. Still others skipped brokering and/or testing entirely or spent minimal time goodwill building.

The source of information distinguishes due diligence and brokerage from goodwill building and testing. Information about trustworthiness gathered from due diligence and brokering comes indirectly from third-party sources; information gathered from goodwill building and testing comes directly from social interaction between potential partners. Some managers we interviewed relied much more heavily on indirect information than did others. For example, some told us they would end the process if references that surfaced from due diligence were poor. However, in making the risky decision to trust, managers ultimately relied on direct information collected during goodwill building or testing – their own judgment, not the judgment of others. Exhibit 1.1 summarizes the key actions that managers used in searching for information to decide to trust.

EXHIBIT 1.1. *Key actions used when searching for trust.*

Action	Definition	Example
Due diligence	The search for archival and reputational information about a potential partner and the company the partner represents. Emphasis for deciding to trust is on others' opinions, relative to archival information.	*What you normally do ... you start to do some pre-check ... to see if any of your current business partners had the chance in the past to deal with the company or person ... and you try to get at least a couple of this kind of references.* (141, Italy)
Brokering	Seeking assurance of the potential partner's trustworthiness via an introduction from a trusted third-party intermediary. Distinct from due diligence because the third-party broker stakes his or her own reputation for trustworthiness on assuring both potential partners of each other's trustworthiness.	*If Mr. B introduces Mr. C to Mr. A, then Mr. A would trust Mr. C, because Mr. A trusts Mr. B, and Mr. A knows that if Mr. C performs very badly, then Mr. B will be very embarrassed and the relationship between Mr. A and Mr. B gets very weak.* (104, Japan)

EXHIBIT 1.1 (*continued*)

Action	Definition	Example
Testing	Getting the potential partner to act or react to a question or statement about which the manager has independent information. Generates firsthand experience to evaluate the trustworthiness of the potential partner.	*I go to my network and ask them about this person, as I go into discussion with this person ... either the input that I got from my network is going to be confirmed or it's going to be questioned. If it ends up questioned, I would say my cautious level will skyrocket.* (113, Palestine)
Goodwill building	Interacting socially for the purpose of getting to know the potential partner. Goodwill building can range from a few minutes of small talk at the beginning of a meeting to extended time spent together in a social context, such as a meal or a football match.	*It's a common thing. People go on like dinners. Maybe the meeting takes like one hour ... but then, let's go on a dinner. And at night they have a couple of drinks, they talk about stuff, life and everything. So they try to get to know each other's character, and so they probably decide there whether to trust that person or not.* (131, Turkey)

CORR Standards for Deciding to Trust

The second set of quotes that open this chapter illustrate the CORR standards (competence, openness, respect, and rapport) that managers used when deciding to trust a potential partner.[6] Competence is the first standard: *It's not like testing I trust you, but testing if you can do it* (103, China). *Sometimes people tell the things they cannot do. It's a big mistake and you lose trust completely. If you are in the industry, you know what's realistic and what's not* (186, Japan). Being competent goes beyond being capable. Competent people are expert, proficient, and qualified. They can complete a task or a project to their partner's satisfaction.

Openness is the second standard: *I think you build trust by sharing information. ... If it's only give, and there's no take, or if there's only a take from his side and no give, then it's not a fair dialog* (127, Germany). People who are open also are honest, objective, forthright, and willing to share information. The verb "to open" means to set in motion, to start, to "get things rolling," which reveals interest in and motivation for the project. In addition, the quote emphasizes give and take. Information sharing is a two-way street; it needs to be reciprocated.

Respect is the third standard: *Everyone can be different ... because people are different usually and you have to respect the choices* (115, Palestine). *If you show that you respect their way of living, etc., can play a big role in smoothing the starting* (102, India). Respect signals regard for another person. People we respect are not necessarily like us but are people whose differences we honor and consider when interacting with them.

Rapport is the last standard: *If you don't know him, find out if he has same values as you do* (157, Brazil). *You have to know the person before you're able to say you trust them* (140, Brazil). People who have rapport have a close and harmonious relationship. They feel an affinity; they share values. Having rapport implies respect, but respect does not necessarily imply rapport, because you can respect people whose values you do not share. When two people have rapport, they not only respect each other's values, they share them. Furthermore, each person's values validate the other's. However, sharing values is not a necessary condition for respecting another person's values. Two people who respect each other but do not share values do not have rapport. Rather their relationship and trust rely on respect – recognition and appreciation of the person's values.

Exhibit 1.2 summarizes the CORR standards our interviewees were using to decide to trust.

EXHIBIT 1.2. *CORR standards used in deciding to trust.*

Standard	Definition	Examples
Competence	Expertise, proficiency, qualifications, track record of completion	*It's not like testing I trust you, but testing if you can do it.* (103, China) *Sometimes people tell things they cannot do. It's a big mistake and you lose trust completely. If you are in the industry, you know what's realistic and what's not.* (186, Japan)

EXHIBIT 1.2 (*continued*)

Standard	Definition	Examples
Openness	Honest, objective, forthright, willing to share information. Also, active, able to set things in motion	*I think you build trust by sharing information. ... If it's only give and there's no take, or if there's only a take from his side and no give, then it's not a fair dialog.* (127, Germany)
Respect	To show regard, honor despite differences	*Everyone can be different ... because people are different usually and you have to respect the choices.* (115, Palestine) *If you show that you respect their way of living, etc., can play a big role in smoothing the starting.* (102, India)
Rapport	Felt affinity and shared values	*If you don't know him, find out if he has same values as you do.* (157, Brazil) *You have to know the person before you're able to say you trust them.* (140, Brazil)

Moving to Cultural Differences in Key Actions and CORR Standards

People use many different standards when deciding to trust[7] and scholars from many different disciplines have studied the determinants, processes, and outcomes of deciding to trust.[8] Our study builds on this prior trust research by recognizing that the context of the trust decision and culture – the norms and values that govern people's everyday social interaction – matters to the way in which people make trust decisions.[9] Our research takes place in a specific context: deciding to trust in a new business relationship. However, our research seeks to understand how culture affects the decision to trust by collecting the experiences of managers from many different national cultures who were responsible for developing new business relationships.

The managers we interviewed were from the four regions of the world – the West, East Asia, Latin America, and the Middle East/South Asia – that the World Bank identifies as the engines of the global economy,[10] which makes these regions relevant to the context of deciding to trust in new business relationships. Although there is significant national diversity within these regions, as we show in the next chapter, people within these regions share culture. In particular, they share a similar level of trust and of tightness-looseness, which refers to the strength of social norms and sanctioning.[11] As we explain in the next chapter, cultural differences in trust and tightness-looseness provide a framework for understanding how managers in different regions were searching for and deciding to trust.

CHAPTER 2

Trust and Tightness-Looseness – Culture and Deciding to Trust

This chapter proposes a simple framework organized by cultural levels of trust and tightness-looseness to explain regional differences in the process of searching for and deciding to trust. It opens by discussing of the role of culture in society. Then, it discusses regional differences in trust (willingness to make yourself vulnerable to another person) and in tightness-looseness (the strength of social norms and tolerance for deviance from them). These regional cultural differences in trust and tightness-looseness form the framework that we introduce in this chapter and use throughout the book both to distinguish the CORR standards people rely on to make the trust decision and the actions they engage in to collect the information they need to make that decision.

How Culture Works

Culture affects people's everyday lives. At the most fundamental level, culture provides functional solutions to problems of social interaction.[1] In other words, different cultures often generate different, but effective, ways

to address the same social problem. Consider greeting someone respectfully. In some cultures, that greeting is a kiss, in others a bow, in others it
is shaking hands, in others one-armed hugs, and in yet others, fist bumps.[2]
The problem is the same – greet respectfully; the solution is different. Is
one culture's manner of greeting better than another culture's? No, just
different.

Why people in different cultures may search for trust differently is
the focus of this chapter. To grasp the nature of these cultural differences, it is helpful to understand more generally how cultures generate
and maintain their differences. To do so we need to learn about cultural
norms.

Cultural norms are the informal rules that guide people's behavior
in group settings. Norms are standards of appropriate behavior. Norms
tell people how they should behave, they allow people to anticipate how
others will behave, and they provide a standard that people can use to
identify what is acceptable and what is deviant behavior.[3] In some cultures, norms are very strong because families, community members, and
governments closely monitor behavior and sanction deviance. Cultural
scholars call these "tight cultures." All cultures have norms, but in other
cultures, norms are weaker, behavior is less closely monitored, and deviance is more frequently tolerated. Cultural scholars call these "loose
cultures."[4]

There is always behavioral variability within culture, although much
more of it in loose than in tight cultures. This means it is useful to think
about a cultural norm as a bell curve.[5] The height and shape of the bell
curve describe two important aspects of the norm as it operates in a
culture. The first is the cultural average. Exhibit 2.1 plots level of trust on
the x-axis and the frequency of people in a culture agreeing to different
levels of trust on the y-axis in two cultures. In exhibit 2.1, the top of the
bell curve for Japan is toward the high-trust end of the x-axis whereas
the top of the bell curve for Brazil lies more toward the low-trust end
of the x-axis. Japan is a higher-trust culture than Brazil.[6] The second is

the cultural variation. Even though levels of trust are quite different in Japan and Brazil, the exhibit shows there is some cultural overlap; not everyone in Brazil has low trust, and not everyone in Japan has high trust. Importantly, Japan's bell curve is also narrower and pointier while Brazil's curve is wider and flatter, indicating that there is less variation of opinion about trust in Japan than there is in Brazil. The degree of in-culture variation illustrates one element of cultural tightness-looseness, the degree to which people share the cultural norm. Japanese culture is tighter than Brazilian culture.

EXHIBIT 2.1. *Culture as a bell curve.*

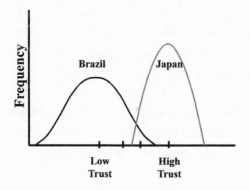

Tightness-looseness plays an important role in our explanation of cultural differences in searching for trust. However, as it may be a less familiar cultural norm than, for example, individualism-collectivism[7] – a cultural norm that distinguishes social interaction in Western and East Asian cultures – we thought an example might be useful. An American (Western, loose culture) manager was posted for two years to Tokyo, Japan (East Asia, tight culture). He and his wife rented a small house in a Japanese, not an expat, neighborhood. He told us that one of their biggest challenges was sorting the recycling correctly.

> *When we first moved in, we were told about the recycling rules, but we couldn't read the brochure. We did our best to sort our recycling, get it into the right bins, to the right pick-up spot, on the right day of the week. We noticed that our neighbors carefully went through our recycling to make sure it was done correctly. They never said anything to us, but they re-sorted where we had made mistakes. We figured out that if we checked on what they'd shifted from one bin to another, we'd learn. After a while, we must have been getting it right, because they stopped checking.*[8]

In a loose culture, close enough is usually good enough. In a tight culture, such as Japan, it isn't. In the example, the Japanese neighbors monitored the quality of the expat family's recycling. In re-sorting it, they also socially sanctioned the expat family. Having your recycling re-sorted by the neighbors is shaming in Japanese society. The family failed to live up to its community responsibility! The American family, however, took the neighbors' re-sorting as an opportunity to learn, not to feel shame, another cultural difference. The Americans also learned the difference between their own loose culture and the tight Japanese culture in which they were living.

Regional Differences

To provide a cultural interpretation of regional differences in the CORR standards people rely on to make the trust decision and the key actions they engage in to search for the information they need to make that decision, we used the cultural characteristics of trust and tightness-looseness. We knew from prior research[9] that these cultural characteristics vary systematically across the four regions of economic activity that we chose to study: Latin America, the Middle East/South Asia, East Asia, and the West. In the next sections, we report analyses revealing systematic regional differences in trust and tightness-looseness.

REGIONAL DIFFERENCES IN TRUST

Trust varies by region. East Asia and the West are high-trust regions, whereas Latin America and the Middle East/South Asia are low-trust regions. We used the World Values Survey measure to test whether trust varies by region. Every five years, since 1981, the World Values Survey[10] asks samples of people across 120 nations a simple question: "Generally speaking, would you say that most people can be trusted or that you need to be very careful in dealing with people?" Choices are "Most people can be trusted," "Don't know," and "Can't be too careful."[11] Although this question has been criticized for being a rather crude estimate of trust, nation-level trust scores from the World Values Survey correlate positively and strongly with other measures of trust.[12] Because the World Values Survey asks the trust question every five years, there is also data showing that the nation-level trust scores correlate over time.[13] This means that trust is stable over time and national differences in trust are meaningful.[14]

Exhibit 2.2 shows that regional differences in trust are also meaningful. The data in exhibit 2.2 are a transformation of national means reported in the World Values Survey.[15] The appendix to this chapter reports the World Values Survey trust percentage and standardized trust percentage for each nation in each region. The exhibit uses the most recent national data available from the World Values Survey. If a nation within the region was not surveyed in Waves 5, 6, or 7, it is not included in the exhibit.

Exhibit 2.2 shows that cultural levels of trust in East Asia and the West are significantly different from cultural levels of trust in Latin America and the Middle East/South Asia.[16] However, there are not statistically significant differences in levels of trust between East Asia and the West

EXHIBIT 2.2. *World Values Survey: Trust at the regional level.*

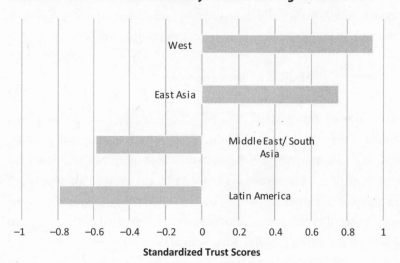

Standardized Trust Scores

or between Latin America and the Middle East/South Asia.[17] Standardization makes it easy to see relative differences between regions. Locate the central zero point on the horizontal axis. This corresponds to the average trust percentage, which was 24 percent, among all the nations included in the exhibit. People in the Latin American and the Middle Eastern/South Asian regions are substantially less trusting than the mean. In contrast, people in the East Asian and Western regions are much more trusting.

ASSETS AND LIABILITIES OF HIGH- AND LOW-TRUST CULTURES

The availability of the World Values Survey trust data motivated a lot of research on why trust is higher in some nations than others. The consensus is that high-trust nations tend to be ethnically homogeneous and historically influenced by Protestant religious traditions. Relative to low-trust nations, high-trust nations also experience wealth (gross domestic product per capita), greater income equality, and good government.[18] Good government refers primarily to government institutions that constrain political leaders to behave in a trustworthy manner, such as division of powers, regular elections, the rule of law, independent judicial oversight, a free press, and freedom of information.

This profile is particularly consistent with high-trust, Western cultures and distinguishes them from ethnically heterogeneous, low-trust, Latin American cultures. Latin American cultures traditionally were influenced by Roman Catholic, not Protestant, religious traditions and do not share the wealth (gross domestic product per capita), income equality, and good government that generally characterize Western culture nations.[19]

Apart from ethnic homogeneity, the high-trust, Western culture profile does not describe high-trust East Asian nations very well and Singapore, a high-trust, East Asian nation, is ethnically extremely diverse. However, as we will see as we move to the next section on tightness-looseness, and especially in chapter 5 devoted to understanding the process of deciding to trust in East Asia, it is cultural tightness, not democratic institutions and Protestant ethic, that imposes constraints leading to trustworthy behavior in that region.

In contrast, low-trust nations in the Middle East, South Asia, and Latin America suffer from income inequality and corruption. The World Values Survey trust index and corruption permissiveness index correlate –.46, indicating that corruption is generally low in high-trust countries.[20] Eric Uslaner, who has studied the relationship between trust and corruption for many years, cautions that the low trust–corruption relationship is not causal but reciprocal; low trust leads to corruption and corruption leads to low trust, and income inequality contributes both to low trust and corruption.[21]

Consider the assets and liabilities of living in a high- versus a low-trust society. In a word, it is easier to live and work in a high- than a low-trust culture because, simply based on statistical probability, you can expect others to be trustworthy. You can expect them to be cooperative and recognize the need to engage in resource sharing. Is there a risk of too much trust? Yes. People may satisfice, that is, accept a good solution when they could generate an excellent solution with little more effort.[22] However, the fact that a high-trust society allows people to take more risks without having to engage in expensive hedging[23] means more social and economic activity. This is a reason why societal trust and economic development go together. Yet economic development happens in low-trust societies, it just happens at a different pace and with different safeguards.

REGIONAL DIFFERENCES IN TIGHTNESS-LOOSENESS

Tightness-looseness varies systematically by region. East Asia and the Middle East/South Asia are tight relative to looser Latin America and the West. We use the Gelfand measure of tightness-looseness to illustrate that some regions are tighter, others looser. The Gelfand measure has six statements reproduced in exhibit 2.3 below. People responding to the survey agree or disagree as to how well each statement describes their culture. The statements refer to the strength of social norms, freedom of action, and monitoring and sanctioning. People's tightness scores are the sum of their answers to the six statements. Tightness scores represent people's view of their cultures, a social description.[24]

EXHIBIT 2.3. *Measuring cultural tightness-looseness.*
- There are many social norms that people are supposed to abide by in this culture.
- In this culture, there are very clear expectations about how people should act in most situations.
- People agree on what behaviors are appropriate versus inappropriate in most situations in this culture.

- People in this culture have a great deal of freedom in deciding how they want to behave in most situations. (reverse coded)
- In this culture, if someone acts in an inappropriate way, others will strongly disapprove.
- People in this culture almost always comply with social norms.

Gelfand and colleagues originally developed their measure of tightness-looseness on a sample of 6823 young adults from 33 nations.[25] Their statistical analyses justify aggregation to the national level.[26] They also present extensive evidence showing that tightness-looseness scores are correlated with other data that reflect higher compliance with norms and intolerance for deviance.[27] For example, data from the World Values Survey show that people who, according to the Gelfand measure, characterize their cultures as tight find socially deviant behavior to be much less justifiable.[28] In 2021, Gelfand and colleagues reported new data collected from people in 57 nations.[29] The correlation between a nation's tightness in old and new data is very high (.87), indicating that like the trust measure, the tightness-looseness measure is stable over time.

The data provided by Gelfand are standardized at the national level. The appendix to this chapter reports the standardized tightness-looseness data for each nation in each region. The exhibit uses the most recent national data published in 2021. If a nation within a region was not in Gelfand's 2021 listing, it was not included in the exhibit.

Exhibit 2.4 shows that cultural levels of tightness in the Middle East/South Asia and East Asia are significantly different from cultural levels of tightness in the West and Latin America.[30] However, there are not statistically significant differences in the level of tightness between the Middle East/South Asia and East Asia or between the West and Latin America.[31] Once again, standardization makes it easy to see relative differences between regions. Locate the central zero point on the horizontal axis. This corresponds to the average tightness among all the nations included in the exhibit. People in the Middle East/South Asia and East Asia regions view their cultures as tight relative to people in the West and Latin America.

EXHIBIT 2.4. *Tightness-looseness at the regional level.*

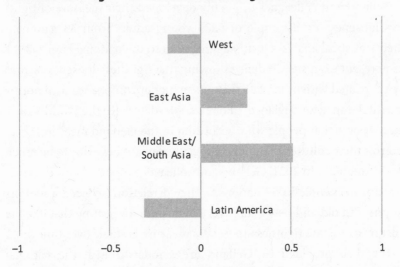

Standardized Tightness-looseness Scores

ASSETS AND LIABILITIES OF TIGHT AND LOOSE CULTURES

Why are some nations and regions tighter than others? The consensus seems to be that tight societies have experienced, in the past and continuing into the present, more severe ecological and human-made threats to survival, for example, high population density, resource scarcity, natural disasters, and territorial threats from competing cultures. To maintain social order in the face of ecological threats, cultures that survive and flourish develop strong norms, engage in substantial social monitoring, and strictly sanction deviant behavior. Strong norms and sanctioning of deviant behavior can be very effective in managing threats. One example is the significantly lower rates of and deaths from COVID-19 in tight compared to loose cultures.[32] Cultures facing fewer ecological threats can survive with less strict social coordination and looser social norms. Looser social norms in turn support a wide range of behavioral options. The upshot is that while tight culture is particularly effective in maintaining social order, loose culture generates more creativity and adaptability.[33]

People's psychological processes adapt to the nature of the culture system in which they live.[34] Cultural tightness-looseness has implications for how people gather and analyze social information concerning the behavior of others, which is highly relevant to our question of how people in different cultures decide to trust. For example, people from tight cultures develop solutions to problems by using cautious, efficient, and disciplined procedures.[35] They are rule makers.[36] Their systematic processes ensure that their decisions thoroughly use available information. This use of systematic pre-existing processes to make decisions means decisions are comprehensive but conservative and so unlikely to challenge social norms. Conversely, individuals from loose cultures develop solutions to problems by challenging normal procedures, ignoring constraints, and searching for answers that go beyond ordinary solutions.[37] They are rule breakers.[38] Their approach is consistent with their loose-culture environment, but both approach and environment put a strong burden on individuals to acquire the skills to reduce the riskiness of everyday decisions.

One other element of cultural tightness-looseness is relevant to our study of regional cultural differences as they relate to cultural differences in the decision to trust. Loose cultures are typically moderately ethnically heterogeneous, but tight cultures can be extremely heterogeneous or extremely homogeneous.[39] Consider tight East Asian cultures, such as Japan, Korea, and China. Citizens of these nations are not particularly ethnically diverse, and each nation has a single dominant language.[40]

People within these homogeneous tight cultures not only share norms but the social and political institutions of their tight national cultures enforce those norms. In contrast, Middle Eastern and South Asian cultures are tight but heterogeneous. Nations within this region consist of many different subcultural groups (tribes, extended families), many of which have different ethnicities, languages, and religions. The evidence in exhibits 2.2 and 2.4 shows that people across subcultures within this region share norms. Across subcultures in this region, trust is low and norms are tight. However, each subculture has its own institutions for monitoring and sanctioning deviant behavior. The social institutions that hold tight cultures together do not necessarily cross subculture boundaries. For example, in heterogeneous, tight cultures, tribal and family elders and religious leaders have authority to monitor and sanction deviant behavior within but not between subcultures. This lack of overall institutional monitoring and sanctioning severely restricts people in heterogeneous, tight cultures from being able to predict the behavior of people outside their own subcultures. The heterogeneous versus homogeneous nature of tight cultures ultimately is going to help us explain differences in the process of deciding to trust in the tight cultures of the Middle East, South Asia, and East Asia.

A Framework for Understanding Cultural Differences in the Trust Decision

The four regions of the world vary with respect to cultural levels of trust and tightness-looseness. As evident from exhibits 2.2 and 2.4, relative to the other three regions, East Asia has a high-trust, tight culture; the Middle East/South Asia has a low-trust, tight culture; Latin America has a low-trust, loose culture; and the West has a high-trust, loose culture. Exhibit 2.5 places the four regions into a cultural framework of trust and tightness-looseness.[41]

We use this "trust by tight-loose framework" throughout the book to explain why there are regional differences in the way that people search for and decide to trust. In the next four chapters we focus on the process of deciding to trust in each region. Just knowing whether a region is high or low trust is not sufficient to understand the process of deciding to trust a potential partner. Understanding the process of deciding to trust requires understanding differences in the nature of trust in tight and loose cultures.

EXHIBIT 2.5. *Regions of trust and tightness-looseness.*

Culture	Low Trust	High Trust
Tight	Middle East/ South Asia (heterogeneous)	East Asia (homogeneous)
Loose	Latin America (moderately heterogeneous)	West (moderately heterogeneous)

This framework defined by cultural levels of trust and tightness-looseness describes the cultural environment in which managers make the decision to trust potential business partners. Each of the next four chapters looks deeply into how that decision to trust occurs in geographically and culturally distinct regions of the world.

Appendix to Chapter 2

Note: Shading distinguishes regions.

Region/ Nation	Tightness standard score[1]	Trust, percent agreeing most people can be trusted[2]	Trust, standard score	Wave of Trust data collection	Region[3]
Argentina	−0.53	19.2	−0.29	7	1
Bolivia		8.5	−0.91	7	1
Brazil	−0.38	6.5	−1.03	7	1

(Continued)

Appendix to Chapter 2 (continued)

Region/ Nation	Tightness standard score[1]	Trust, percent agreeing most people can be trusted[2]	Trust, standard score	Wave of Trust data collection	Region[3]
Chile	−0.34	12.9	−0.66	7	1
Colombia	−0.58	4.5	−1.14	7	1
Ecuador	−0.18	5.8	−1.07	7	1
Guatemala		18	−0.36	7	1
Mexico	−0.35	10.5	−0.80	7	1
Nicaragua		4.2	−1.16	7	1
Peru	−0.34	4.2	−1.16	7	1
Portugal[4]	0.1				1
Spain[4]	−0.3	19	−0.31	6	1
Trinidad and Tobago	−0.2	14	−0.59	7	1
Algeria	0.69	17.2	−0.41	6	2
Armenia	0.21	10.9	−0.77	6	2
Egypt		7.3	−0.98	7	2
India	0.73	16.7	−0.44	6	2
Indonesia	0.5	4.6	−1.14	7	2
Iran	0.38	14.8	−0.55	7	2
Iraq		11	−0.77	7	2
Jordan		15.9	−0.48	7	2
Lebanon		9.9	−0.83	7	2
Malaysia	0.22	19.6	−0.27	7	2
Pakistan		23.3	−0.06	7	2
Qatar	0.85	21.4	−0.17	6	2
Saudi Arabia	0.62				2
Sri Lanka	0.65				2
Tunisia		13.8	−0.61	7	2
Turkey	0.29	11.6	−0.73	6	2
UAE	0.48				2
China	0.19	63.5	2.26	7	3
Japan	0.19	33.7	0.54	7	3
Singapore	0.36	37.3	0.75	6	3
South Korea	0.19	32.9	0.50	7	3
Thailand	0.25	28.9	0.27	7	3
Vietnam	0.39	27.7	0.20	7	3
Australia	−0.05	48.5	1.39	7	4
Austria	0.21				4
Canada	−0.14	41.8	1.01	5	4
Czech Republic	−0.46				4

(Continued)

Appendix to Chapter 2 (continued)

Region/ Nation	Tightness standard score[1]	Trust, percent agreeing most people can be trusted[2]	Trust, standard score	Wave of Trust data collection	Region[3]
Estonia	−0.47	39	0.85	6	4
Finland	−0.28	58	1.94	5	4
Germany	0.13	44.6	1.17	7	4
Greece	−0.28	8.4	−0.92	7	4
Hungary	−0.6	28.7	0.25	5	4
Iceland	0.04				4
Ireland	−0.18				4
Italy	−0.06	27.5	0.18	5	4
Netherlands	−0.54	66.1	2.41	6	4
New Zealand		56.6	1.86	7	4
Poland	−0.32	22.2	−0.12	6	4
Sweden	0.34	60.1	2.06	6	4
United Kingdom	−0.21	30	0.33	5	4
United States	−0.13	37	0.73	7	4

[1] Gelfand, M.J., Jackson, J.C., Pan, X., Nau, D., Pieper, D., Denison, E., ... Wang, M. (2021). The relationship between cultural tightness–looseness and COVID-19 cases and deaths: A global analysis. *The Lancet Planetary Health, 5*(3), e135–e144.

[2] Inglehart, R., Haerpfer, C., Moreno, A., Welzel, C., Kizilova, K., Diez-Medrano, J., Lagos, M., Norris, P., Ponarin, E., Puranen, B., et al., (Eds.). (2014). *World Values Survey: All Rounds – Country-Pooled Datafile Version*: www.worldvaluessurvey.org/ WVSDocumentationWVL.jsp. Madrid: JD Systems Institute.

[3] 1 = Latin America, 2 = Middle East/South Asia, 3 = East Asia, 4 = West

[4] We classified Spain and Portugal with Latin America rather than Europe and the West because of the strong cultural ties between these two European countries and their former colonies. These ties include but are not limited to religion and language.

CHAPTER 3

Middle East and South Asia – Respect Rules

- *Building trust takes time. You may not want to trust people at the beginning.* (177, India)
- *You need to be conscious of a lot of cultural norms, given that there's so much diversity.* (146, UAE)

In deciding to trust, managers in the Middle East and South Asia followed a systematic process to learn about the person they were considering as a potential business partner. They relied primarily on three of the four key actions to generate information to make the trust decision. These were due diligence (conducting a background check about the person's reputation); brokering (being introduced to the person in question by a person you trust); and, especially, goodwill building (engaging in a rather extended social interaction to assess the person's respect for cultural differences). Testing was not a key action in this region, and when we asked about its role in the process of deciding to trust, managers said they would be concerned that doing so would make them appear untrustworthy. The primary standard for making the decision to trust in the Middle East and South Asia was respect for cultural differences.

A cultural environment of low trust and heterogeneous tightness-looseness explains the process of searching for and deciding to trust in this region and structures our advice for this region.

Due Diligence and Brokering Are Key Early Actions

In this region, the first step in the process of deciding whether to trust involves due diligence, specifically, seeking references of good character. As several interviewees explained:

- *Most of our business runs through references. Then we start talking to that person who gave the reference and say, "Hey, can you give us some more data about this?"* (178, India)
- *Basically, you talk to a few people, you get some sort of an idea about this guy, how he operates, how trustworthy he is, how greedy he is when it comes to doing business. I talk to other people in the community ... ask them about him, about whether I should move forward or not* (113, Palestine)
- *You don't get the job because you're the best, you get the job because you know someone, and this is the base of the whole culture ... people just take care of people who know each other. So it's like a tribal thing.* (131, Turkey)

Information gathered via due diligence is highly valued because there is an expectation that people will give truthful information about potential partners: *People don't keep secrets here, so they tell you everything* (115, Palestine). Negative information about the potential partner brings the process to a halt before too much time and effort have been invested: *We're looking for no negatives, illegal experiences* (146, UAE). *If I find something which is clearly negative, his trustworthiness is not good, his past business dealings are not good* (177, India). *If the reputation is negative about somebody, it serves as a quick filter to disregard consid-ering that party as a possible counterpart for a transaction or a partner* (136, Saudi Arabia).

In contrast, because a reputation for integrity is relatively rare in this region, positive information is highly valued although subject to confir-mation: *In a society where trust is very low, to build a reputation takes a lot of effort* (102, India). Managers typically did not rely on a single pos-itive reference: *So if there's a good reputation, that's good, but let's recheck it* (131, Turkey). *You should double-check or ask more than one person. I have to make sure that it's the same description or advice from more than one person* (101, Kuwait).

In this region, brokering is especially valued because a third-party broker, whom you trust and who trusts your potential partner, puts him- or herself on the line by making an introduction. If the person introduced by the broker ultimately fails to be trustworthy, the relation-ship with the broker also will be compromised, creating a strong incen-tive for the broker only to introduce parties whom the broker trusts.

- *It matters that the introduction is getting made from somebody you trust.* (169, India)
- *Culturally, we think that if I trust a person … they wouldn't do wrong to me, so if this person brings a new partner to me, then he (new part-ner) is one that I can trust.* (135, Turkey)
- *So through their trust, they trust me. And because of that trust, I feel obligated to do my job in my best way, because if I lose that client, I wouldn't be losing that client only, but also my former client or my friend or the one who trusted me before. You can only lose trust once. Then it spreads like a plague.* (131, Turkey)

These quotes about the importance of brokering in searching for information to use in deciding to trust are consistent with research suggesting that brokers can positively influence trust by promoting cooperation.[1] However, brokers can also exacerbate an already negative relationship if what they say increases people's suspicions of each other. The major limitation on brokering in this region, however, is finding a broker who knows and can vouch for both partners. Recall from chapter 2 that there are many subcultures within this region. Since subcultural boundaries are not very permeable, it may be challenging to find someone with the relationships needed to be a broker in both subcultures.

Goodwill Building to Establish a Personal Relationship

Just having a good reputation or a brokered introduction is not enough information to trust a potential partner in the Middle East/South Asia. Managers wanted to meet the potential partner in person. One told us, *I've had experiences where their reputation looked great, their profile looked great, but the people were very different* (180, India). Another made the same point: *I would always want to meet that person* (177, India). Managers explained that although initial judgments might be based on family background, *sometimes we do judge people on their backgrounds* (115, Palestine), there was still a question of whether the individual merited trust.

> *And face-to-face interaction is important to tell if the reputation was based on family history, rather than personal attributes to that person. And so some of that is checking whether this particular individual who is part of a family that's well known for, let's say a good business interaction, is following the same path or not. And this is back to this tribal society where it's you and your family reputation. You know, it's not really independent.* (101, Kuwait)

These in-person meetings typically were held in a social setting; yet goodwill building is more than a "getting to know you" encounter – it is an opportunity to actively assess the character of the other person (that is, their level of respect). For example, managers we interviewed explained that they could signal respect by offering hospitality and judge respect by how graciously others accepted it.

- *People go on like dinners, they have a couple drinks, they talk about stuff, life and everything. So, they try to get to know each other's character.* (131, Turkey)
- *You're not purposefully trying to negotiate a contract. That usually does not happen over dinner.* (177, India)
- *If you show respect by trying to wear the local attire, greeting the person in the local manner, showing that you respect their way of living, etc., can play a big role in smoothing the starting.* (102, India)
- *We like hospitality. You should show some generosity, so people feel that you are generous to them and you're willing to give.* (195, Saudi Arabia)
- *I recognize it's the presence, how I come across, how I accommodate them, and the hospitality is extremely critical.* (133, Lebanon)
- *If I'm visiting and the other person said, "Okay, we'll take you out for some good places to eat." So that because the person is committing time (to host us), we feel it (that commitment) applies to the connection (between us).* (177, India)

Hospitality and Respect

Managers in the Middle East and South Asia relied strongly on courteously offered and graciously received hospitality as a signal of respect. Respect is the ultimate standard for trust in this region; hence, the theme of this chapter is respect rules. We heard about respect over and over again as we talked with people from this region. Some examples are in exhibit 3.1.

EXHIBIT 3.1. *Respect rules in the Middle East/South Asia.*

- *So, while I'm keeping my traditions, I'm accepting yours.* (101, Kuwait)
- *Everyone can be different, because people are different usually and you have to respect the choices.* (115, Palestine)
- *If you are having a meeting with somebody and then he excuses himself because he wants to go pray, this is normal. You have to accept that this is the culture in our region.* (182, Jordan)
- *When you meet somebody senior, double your age, they would like it if you touch their feet. Touching feet is seeking blessing. Namaste is still a good greeting. Dressing conservatively is good. People accept that people from across the world can bring different cultures, but* (showing respect) *they would like that.* (177, India)
- *If you find that you're different (I'm talking about political issues), then you have to evaluate the business deal. Is it okay to do business with people with these kinds of concepts or not? If it's okay, then you don't care how they see things and everyone can be different.* (115, Palestine)

One manager we interviewed told us a long story illustrating the importance of hospitality but also respect. An ambassador was attending a social event at a host's home. (Our interviewee was a guest.) The ambassador brought his armed security detail into the room. The host asked the ambassador to dismiss his security or at least have them take their guns outside. The ambassador complied. The interviewee explained: *So the key was each party respected the other even though really strong differences* (among other things about the appropriateness of bringing a security detail to a social event) (101, Kuwait).

On the other hand, testing (i.e., asking a question to which you already know the answer), although common in some regions, was not common in the Middle East/South Asia. Testing was not raised spontaneously in our first round of interviews, so we asked about testing in some of the later interviews. One person responded thoughtfully: *Play a trick on them by asking a question that I know the answer of? I don't think I would do that, unless I feel they are really not being truthful* (136, Saudi Arabia). The second half of this quote suggests that the interviewee thought that testing could risk his own reputation by signaling distrust. Recall from the prior quote: *In a society where trust is very low, to build a reputation takes a lot of effort* (102, India) – our interviewee was concerned about risking his own reputation.

Competence, a major concern in East Asia, was also a concern in this region, but it was mentioned much less often than respect. Managers told us they did not take the potential partner's competence for granted. Indeed, they were often wary when a potential partner expressed too much confidence in his own competence.

- *If a company tries to tell me, "Hey guys, we work 24/7 and we can do everything for you. We can take care of your needs." I know that's not true. "Guys let's be realistic. I'm not expecting you to work 24/7. Give me an example, give me a case study where you guys have done a project, And then let's talk after that."* (178, India)
- *He said, "You're not even seeing the full picture. Our company is doing even better than that." And I said, "I'm looking at your financials. It's doing okay, but what do you mean it's doing better?" He said, "Well this is only the reported income." So right away, I was leaving that deal.* (136, Saudi Arabia)
- *It's important to kind of know that that person's not coming in cocky into the discussion.* (133, Lebanon)

People from the Middle East and South Asia interpreted overstatements and overconfidence as indicators that a potential partner should not be trusted. One of our interviewees told us about looking for a broker to make an introduction. When he started talking to the potential broker, he realized the broker was a braggart and could not be trusted. *Because he was totally bragging. For example, I checked his social media. There were only pictures of himself, his face, and his cars, glamorous life, but it was a show-off. He immediately started to talk about how much money he should make and stuff like that, so we didn't trust the guy* (131, Turkey).

The Middle East/South Asia: Low-trust, Heterogeneous, Tight Culture

Because of the intersection of low trust and cultural tightness, deciding to trust a potential new partner in the Middle East and South Asia is a risky endeavor,[2] particularly if the new relationship crosses a subcultural boundary.[3] Subcultures, although sharing the characteristic of cultural tightness, do not share the same mechanisms for monitoring and sanctioning deviant behavior. The combination of a low-trust environment and lack of social monitoring and sanctioning means that people are unlikely to assume that others who are not members of their subculture will be trustworthy. The managers we interviewed in the Middle Eastern/South Asian region confirmed that their region was low trust, heterogeneous, and tight. They described a cautious, systematic approach to the process of deciding to trust – goodwill building during which they were seeking evidence of respect.

When we asked managers about whether people would trust a new potential partner, their answers were uniformly wary:

- *I've been burnt before, (there's an) everybody's out to get me kind of mindset.* (133, Lebanon)
- *As (in) most of the Middle East, I don't think that anyone can say that most of the people can (be trusted).* (115, Palestine)

- *People are typically not very trusting towards each other. There's always a bit of skepticism.* (180, India)
- *You cannot assume that they're trustworthy people. There's a lot of people who take advantage of people.* (131, Turkey)

Managers we talked to from the Middle East/South Asia assumed that people they did not know could not be trusted. When people assume others are not trustworthy, their behavior follows their assumption. Think about what you do when you don't trust someone. Do you act the same way you would if you trusted them? Of course, you don't. Our assumptions about trust are reflected in our behaviors, and others pick up on this. If I'm signaling, I don't trust you, why would you in turn act as though you trust me?

When we asked managers in this region about the strength of cultural norms, they not only told us about important norms, such as respect for hierarchy, but also about the social pressure that encouraged conformity to social norms.

- *It's a traditional country in terms of how the young people should behave and how the older people should behave.* (117, Turkey)
- *I assume you know that the Arabic people have so many customs that control the everyday treatment, everyday ethics.* (115, Palestine)
- *Well, in my country, there is a huge social pressure on everything. There's always a way to do things, and if you don't follow, then you will feel the social pressure. It can be a woman's appearance, or it can be the way to greet people or the way you do business. The social pressure takes a bigger part than the laws.* (131, Turkey)

When we asked, "What happens if people break the norms?" one manager told us, *It doesn't go down well, so it could hurt your relationship* (146, UAE). This person advised, *(You have) to ensure that you come across as sincere, as honest, and as sensitive to the local cultural nuances.* He gave us an example, *A lot of women in business, for instance, would not shake hands with you. You need to know that. If you offer to shake hands with the CEO of a business who happens to be a lady, then you've sort of already dug a hole for yourself at the start, just by doing something that is very normal and, in fact, the accepted norm in many parts of the world* (146, UAE).

The Middle East/South Asia is tight but diverse, consisting of many subcultures. Managers, in talking to us about the importance of respect in this region, emphasized these differences. One said, *What is different to how things work in the other parts of the world is the importance of being sensitive to the cultural norms. That is something which requires special emphasis and effort* (146, UAE). Another manager was explicit about the difficulty in cross subculture boundaries to do business: *Saudi Arabia is very much a country that people come from different regions and from different tribes. Business can be very easy if these two people are coming from the same tribe. If they come from different ones, or sometimes opponent ones, then this can make it very difficult* (195, Saudi Arabia).

As we pointed out previously, although subcultures in heterogeneous, tight cultures may share norms, they do not share the institutions that monitor and sanction deviance from normative behavior. The social structures that hold the tight culture together don't cross subculture barriers. People have to find out for themselves whether people from subcultures are trustworthy.

Low trust, heterogeneity, and tightness explain the key actions managers in this region used to generate information they needed to decide to trust and the CORR standard, respect, they used to evaluate that information. Managers engaged in significant due diligence, searching for data as well as others' experiences and opinions of the reputations of potential partners. Most importantly, however, managers engaged in goodwill building. These in-person meetings were opportunities to offer hospitality and judge respect prior to opening substantive work conversations. We see this systematic process of information gathering as consistent with the cautious, efficient, and disciplined procedures characteristic of decision making in tight cultures.[4] Low trust motivated the search for multiple references revealing no negative information. Brokered introductions were highly valued but, in this heterogeneous, tight region, finding a broker who had experience with both parties to the potential new relationship was not always possible. The final decision to trust across tight boundaries distinguishing families, tribes, religions, and politics relied on respect being demonstrated and reciprocated during the goodwill building stage of social interaction. Goodwill building is a safe social environment for both parties to signal their own and monitor the other's respect for differences. Respect indicates a commitment to honor someone from a different subculture, as one would honor another within one's own subculture, even in the absence of the social monitoring and sanctioning that maintains harmony within subcultures. For all these reasons, respect ruled the trust decision in low-trust, heterogeneous, tight Middle Eastern and South Asian cultures.

Advice on Developing New Business Relationships in the Middle East and South Asia

If you are from a culture in the Middle Eastern/South Asian region, you are likely to be familiar with what we learned about the process of developing trust in new business relationships in this region. The cultural explanation of this process may be new to you and keeping in mind that this is a region of low trust and heterogeneous tightness-looseness may be helpful to you and to others not from this region in searching for and deciding to trust in the Middle East and South Asia. Based on our research, we offer several recommendations to help build trusting relationships with potential partners in this region.

- Identify someone who has worked with the potential partner to introduce you or provide a character reference.

- You are probably going to need multiple positive references about your character.
- Try to set up an in-person meeting.
- Find out the local norms (greeting, attire) and demonstrate awareness and respect. People expect cultural differences but demonstrating knowledge of and respect for local norms can help a lot in establishing trustworthiness. Remember, these norms may vary from country to country in a heterogeneous region like the Middle East/ South Asia, so don't make the mistake of assuming that the local norms can be generalized across the region.
- Expect those early meetings to have a social element to them. Recognize that even though the occasion is social, you are being evaluated as a potential business partner. Show respect!
- Take tea, have a coffee, and share a meal together. Be gracious accepting hospitality and offering hospitality in return.
- Respect cultural norms. For example, you don't have to pray when they do, but you should respect their doing so.
- Be patient. The trust process takes time in the Middle East/South Asia. Don't expect the other person to trust you initially.
- Demonstrate humility and not haughtiness. Over-emphasizing your own or your company's achievements is likely to make people cautious about trusting you.

Moving on to High-trust, Loose Culture

In this chapter, we saw how managers from the Middle East/South Asia navigate the barriers of low trust, heterogeneity, and tightness to make the decision to trust a potential new partner. In the next chapter, focusing on Latin America, we will see how a culture of low trust and looseness affects the process of deciding to trust a potential partner. You might think that when trust is low, loose culture – a lack of strong social norms and strong institutions monitoring and sanctioning deviance – would make the process of deciding to trust even more difficult than in a heterogeneous, tight culture. However, as we will see in the next chapter, loose culture can facilitate the process of deciding to trust a potential partner. To be sure, low trust is a more challenging starting point than high trust, but loose culture has some surprising features that facilitate deciding to trust.

CHAPTER 4

Latin America – Rapport Is a Requirement

- *(You) build trust with (a) person if you have that emotional link.* (157, Brazil)
- *In fact, our norms are not that rigid in terms of social behavior or social interactions.* (145, Brazil)

In Latin America, the decision to trust depends on rapport. The logic is that people are less likely to violate trust if they have a personal relationship based on shared values and worldview. Latin American managers relied primarily on two of the four actions that we identified as key to searching for trust: due diligence and goodwill building. They relied less on brokering and in general did not engage in testing others to check for truthfulness. Judging from our interviews, managers in this region depended heavily on goodwill building to judge rapport, their ultimate standard for trust.

Due Diligence and Brokering

Our Latin American interviewees sought indirect information about a potential partner's character via due diligence.

- *It's a culture where you value a lot the opinion of the social environment. For example, if you wanted to do business with me, I would ask
  around if someone knows you and has already done some work with
  you. That opinion might be very important for me to have more trust
  in the beginning of our discussion.* (144, Bolivia)
- *Seek references from people you know, who know the person.* (140,
  Brazil)
- *Maybe use Facebook or Twitter because most of the time you can find
  personal values in that kind of research.* (137, Mexico)

They frankly admitted that negative information that turns up in due
diligence is fatal to their decision to trust the person they're seeking information about. *If you heard one guy wants to make an alliance with
you, and three or four shareholders say that he's very corrupt and he doesn't
comply with his word, that's very important, because if he stole from other
guys, the most probable thing is he will do it to you* (190, Mexico). When
we asked if they would decline to move ahead when a reference was un-
enthusiastic, one interviewee told us, *I think yes* (would not move ahead),
*because if you are talking with people that you know very well and they give
you this kind of feedback, you don't want to take the risk* (183, Uruguay).

Interviewees told us that they would use brokering, but only if the
broker was someone they trusted.

- *Only if I trust this person who introduced us.* (181, Peru)
- *If you have a recommendation from a friend and you trust your
  friend, then you most likely will trust that other person that you just
  meet.* (170, Ecuador)
- *If somebody introduces you to each other, that sets up almost like an
  expectation of that business is going to happen.* (179, Chile)

Unfortunately, we also heard some horror tales of brokers who introduced partners who ultimately did not work out. *I was looking for an*

investment in Colombia and a friend recommended someone (a broker) *to help.* (working with the broker) *We came up with a okay possibility and moved some money into this business. But at the end I realized that this person* (the broker) *was getting a commission and it wasn't the best investment. I lost money* (160, Colombia). Our interviewee went on to say that the only reason he followed the broker's advice was that his friend had recommended the broker and that with this experience he learned not to make the same mistake.

Assess for Shared Values and Build Rapport

Although our Latin American interviewees said they used due diligence to collect information about potential partners indirectly, as all the quotes in exhibit 4.1 illustrate, but goodwill building required meeting in person. They were using goodwill building to see if they could form a social relationship, not a business relationship. *Go out with them socially, need to make a connection* (125, Ecuador). *Engage in social contact – no business talk* (119, Nicaragua).

EXHIBIT 4.1. *Goodwill building to generate rapport.*
- *Because here in Colombia, we are affective people, if you are too cold, if you are just a businessman, if your clients think that you're just selling them a solution, but you don't care about them, I think that will be ice in the process.* (124, Colombia)
- *The small talking in Latin America is very important. A good way that we've found to do it is by sharing a meal. We try not to talk business, we just get to meet each other, get to see if we have things in common. Most of the times, we do. We stay off topic for a couple hours during*

*breakfast or lunch. When you have a full stomach, you can have a
longer meeting.* (109, Mexico)
- *I think for most of the Americans that I deal with in my company, they
  are sometimes, "I hate to go to Brazil or Mexico, because you get there,
  you have to kiss the whole department and say hi to everybody. And
  I'm missing like 30 minutes of my day just doing that." But for us, that's
  fine. You're building trust with the person as well if you somehow have
  this emotional link.* (157, Brazil)
- *Taking them to a sports match or a soccer game is very possible.
  That will generate a lot of trust if they actually know about it, too.*
  (125, Ecuador)
- *First meeting … even if you talk about business, you will enter in more
  personal details and probably after three or four meetings you will be
  able to say, okay, these guys, I can trust these guys.* (147, Mexico)
- *A meeting could take two, three hours and then you can start talking
  about the business, but the conversation will be driven to another
  topic and then you have to come back again to the business, it's not a
  straightforward meeting usually.* (170, Ecuador)

In Latin America, trust depended on rapport and rapport rested on
shared values. There was more than just relationship building going
on during goodwill building. Managers in Latin America were using
goodwill building as an opportunity to judge character. They were particularly interested in the potential partner's values, especially concerning family, and they used goodwill building to assess those values.

*When you're talking about your family, about something that you
like talking about even if you try very, very hard, you cannot hide
yourself for the whole two hours. There will be like five minutes
where you're going to show your true colors, right? That's what you*

want to see. Are they open? Are they transparent? Or are they shady?
Are they suspicious? Like, their true self, the one that you're going to
be working with. (179, Chile)

Managers drew inferences about shared values from what potential
partners said they did. For example, *Every Sunday I have lunch with my*
grandmother. This tells you a lot about that person, you know, about respect.
You can see if this person is proud about his family or not (183, Uruguay).
They also drew inferences about shared values from observing the potential partner interacting with others. *Just how he treats others also is very im-*
portant. Is he respectful to the waiter or not. If he's rude to the waiter, that tells
me that probably he thinks that he deserves everything, and if he's working
with me, then he's going to try do things his way too much (119, Nicaragua).

Ultimately, the decision to trust in this region came down to a feeling
of rapport: *It's more a perception of the person, how he reacts and what*
he says, and how much he shares. It's a lot of a feeling. Not something that
you see (187, Mexico). If the potential partner did not share the manager's personal values, there was great reluctance to move ahead with a
business relationship. *Find out if (they) have same values as you do* (157,
Brazil). *I would say if you perceive that values are not shared, that is where*
you decide if things can continue in a good way or if you feel not really
willing to have the next conversation (144, Bolivia).

The reason shared values were so important to managers in Latin
American is that they assumed that people who were like them could
be trusted. They were very reluctant to trust people who did not share
their values.

- *I think that we have like a special connection ... and I think that it's*
  similar to me, it's more probable that I trust them. (124, Colombia)
- *I think that you first try to know with whom you are interacting*
  and based on that knowledge, you start building an idea of how
  trustworthy this person can or cannot be, and you usually do this by

understanding social interactions or social connections that you can have with this person or company. (144, Bolivia)

When we asked one interviewee what happens if you find out that you don't share values, she told us, *You would probably just keep up with the meeting but then after that person leaves, you already know, okay we are not doing a deal with this person* (170, Ecuador).

Another interviewee told us two memorable stories that illustrate how, in some cases, having a personal relationship and rapport can even be more important than business credentials. His first story:

My company is a minority shareholder in a joint venture with several other partners. When there was an opportunity for a contract that would benefit all of the joint venture partners, everyone wanted me to be running the negotiations on behalf of everyone. That has two aspects. First, they (joint venture partners) *trusted me as a good professional, but at the same time, they trusted me as a person because they know me. They know that that I build strong relationships.* (145, Brazil)

His second story:

I'm starting a new venture as a publisher. I'm doing it with a friend of mine. We worked from scratch on building a new company. That was completely different from what I'm used to, because I usually work for companies that have good structure, they know what they do, they have standards. We didn't have anything. So, instead of standards, I relied on the fact that my partner was a good guy, and he was try-ing to do his best. So our personal relationship was important. That we share the same principles, that's good enough. I haven't tested his credentials in terms of being a businessman. We worked much more in terms of understanding that we share the same values. That is very much aligned with what happens in Latin America. (145, Brazil)

As highlighted in the stories above and the quotes that precede it, in Latin America, deciding to trust was all about assessing values and building rapport. Testing was not commonly used: *Once you have decided to do business, it's because you have some level of trust already; you are not checking anymore* (170, Ecuador).

Cultural Explanation: Low Trust and Cultural Looseness

In low-trust, loose cultures such as in Latin America, managers built rapport to insulate themselves against being exploited in a new business relationship. A low-trust, loose culture implies that the society has neither institutional systems (e.g., rule of law) nor social systems (e.g., social monitoring and sanctioning) that are strong enough to protect people from exploitation by others. In this environment, managers engaged in extensive goodwill building to generate rapport, assuming that shared values minimize the risk of exploitation by the potential partner.

The managers we talked to in this region confirmed their cultural characterization by the World Values Survey as low trust. When we asked, "Will people trust a new potential business partner?" answers were uniformly wary:

- *No!* (laughter). (125, Ecuador)
- *Usually not, being very honest.* (145, Brazil)
- *Definitely not!* (179, Chile)
- *Be really reluctant to trust the people. You have to be careful because in this culture (because of) the corruption, you have to pick really well the people that you're willing to trust.* (160, Colombia)
- *No, because I think there is a lot of corruption right now in my country, unfortunately, so you have to be very careful.* (147, Mexico)
- *I would say that no, you will not start by trusting someone if you don't know him.* (132, Panama)

- *No, we have a history of always trying to take advantage (of) people.* (181, Peru)

One Latin American interviewee told us that even when he sold a car to his own brother, he was not entirely certain he could trust him.

> *I sold my car to my brother for a specific amount of money. And, we discussed that at the dinner table with my father near me. You would think that the buyer being my brother, it would only be necessary to reach agreement and shake hands, but here in our culture you need to double check. There is a saying in my culture, "You can trust somebody but you may not put your hand in the fire for him." So, my brother, I love him, I trust him, but in business you don't know how a person can react in certain specific moments of his life.* (181, Peru)

The story and quotes above clearly illustrate that Latin Americans do not enter into new business relationships assuming the other person, even a family member, can be trusted. Why is this? Cultural looseness provides one explanation. Here is the question we asked about cultural tightness-looseness: "Are there many social norms that people are supposed to abide by?" Our interviewees recognized that some Latin American national cultures were looser than others, but their main point was that Latin American culture was loose in general, which is consistent with the most recent research data presented in exhibit 2.4. Interviewees told us:

- *It used to be that way, but now it's changing and it's a little different than in the past.* (147, Mexico)
- *For example, getting a divorce is not something culturally accepted … but then once you get it and time passes, people just forget about it.* (170, Ecuador)

Our Latin American interviewees were open about the corruption that plagued their societies. They recognized there were few social sanctions in their cultures for behavior that violated norms and, as a result, that they could not rely on their governments to confront specific instances of corruption. In this low-trust cultural environment, it makes total sense to spend considerable time deciding to trust, which Latin Americans did.

Experience in low-trust, loose culture may facilitate the process of deciding to trust. In such an environment, people interact frequently with others whom they cannot assume are trustworthy. This means they constantly use their skills to decide if others can be trusted. The friendly, get-to-know you, goodwill building that the managers we interviewed described is not unique to business interactions in Latin America.[1] This is the how Latin Americans handle their low-trust social environment. Consider the difference between the everyday experiences of Latin Americans and Middle Easterners/South Asians. In their everyday social and business lives, Middle Easterners and South Asians interact with people within their own subcultures, people whom they can trust because of cultural tightness. In contrast, in their everyday social and business lives, Latin Americans interact with people whom they have little reason to trust. This makes everyday social interaction more difficult, but it also gives people a lot of practice deciding to trust.

Why is rapport so important in Latin America but not respect, which is so prized in Middle Eastern/South Asian cultures? We believe this is related to the difference between the moderately heterogeneous, but loose, Latin American cultures and the strongly heterogeneous, but tight, Middle Eastern/South Asian cultures. There are certainly subcultures in Latin America. However, in modern history, they have coexisted more harmoniously than the subcultures in Middle Eastern and South Asian cultures. Michele Gelfand, who has researched cultural tightness-looseness extensively, writes that cultural tightness makes good evolutionary sense in societies with histories of chronic threat, such as natural disasters, disease, famine, or war. Such societies develop strict rules to protect order and promote cohesion.[2] The violence between religious groups that continues to plague the Middle East and South Asia (in particular, between Muslims and Hindus, Muslims and Jews, and Sunni and Shia) generally has not been experienced recently in Latin America. Differences in Latin America are not so starkly drawn and so are potentially easier to bridge than in the Middle East and South Asia. Rapport, the core value in Latin America, rests on similarities. In contrast, respect, the core value in the Middle East/South Asia, rests on recognizing and honoring differences. Nevertheless, in both these low-trust regions, reliance on extensive goodwill building to establish whether values are shared or different values are respected is a functional way to decide to trust, even if time consuming and not foolproof.

Advice on Developing New Business Relationships in Latin America

If you are from a culture in the Latin American region, you are likely to be familiar with what we learned about the process of developing trust in new business relationships. The cultural explanation of this process may be new to you but keeping in mind that this is a region of low trust and cultural looseness may be helpful to you and to others not from this region in searching for and deciding to trust in Latin America. Based on our research, we offer several recommendations to help build trusting relationships with potential partners in this region.

- Get references from people you know, who know the person.
- Be prepared to commit time to building a personal relationship in social activities.
- Don't be afraid to talk about your personal values and beliefs or your family. This type of information is welcomed in conversations in Latin America because people trust based on shared values.

- Attend a social event with the other person (e.g., soccer game). Showing interest in or knowledge of the sport, music, or art can help even more.
- Share a meal together and be ok with the fact that you may spend hours talking about things other than business.
- If you plan to get someone to broker an introduction, make sure the person is someone you trust highly.

Moving to High-Trust Culture

Having developed insight into the process of deciding to trust in two low-trust regions of the world, we now turn to the process as it occurs in high-trust cultures. As we will see in the next two chapters, first in East Asia and then in the West, a high-trust culture makes a fundamental difference in the process of deciding to trust. People in both regions can assume that others are trustworthy. Nevertheless, managers in East Asia and the West approached searching for trust rather differently. Tightness-looseness provides an explanation for why.

CHAPTER 5

East Asia – Trustworthy, Competent, Adherent

When I do a face-to-face (meeting) with you, I can ask questions directly, and I can then see whether you actually know what your company is doing and whether you can give me confidence that you as a boss of your company can run the project efficiently and deliver. (174, Hong Kong)

The dominant CORR standard for deciding to trust in East Asia is competence, as expressed in the opening quote. However, determining competence is a middle step in the structured East Asian process of deciding to trust. The first step is brokering. East Asians also engage in due diligence, particularly using information about the status of their potential partner's university or company as a proxy for initial evidence of trustworthiness. Brokering, however, is the preferred method of vetting a potential partner because confidence in the broker swiftly propels East Asians to the in-person stage of testing for competence. The opening quote illustrates that testing for competence focuses on whether the potential partner's organization can deliver the project. Once past the competency hurdle, East Asians are likely to engage in goodwill building to celebrate the forthcoming project, but goodwill building in East Asia is also an opportunity to test for adherence to social norms.

A Brokered Introduction: The Key First Act

In East Asia, a brokered introduction is the preferred way to meet a potential business partner. East Asians have turned the practice into a fine art.

- *To be introduced can make people more trustworthy in Japan.* (118, Japan)
- *So, the first thing is who introduced us.* (134, Korea)
- *If the referral company already knows me, then he will provide me genuine feedback on what his clients are.* (174, Hong Kong)
- *Because even if I have doubting, and even I feel uncomfortable, I'll still believe the person who introduced us, I'll keep going.* (129, Korea)
- *If the person who introduces this guy to me has a very good credit, then I can trust him. His friend should also be a really good guy. But if the person doing the introduction is a bad guy, and he introduces us, there will be problems. This is because Chinese people think that people who work together/are friends have same character.* (161, China)
- *The more efficient way is to get someone to introduce so they are putting their own credits in and people will trust each other very quickly.* (176, China)

All of these quotes illustrate just how much weight managers in East Asia place on an introduction by a trusted third party. The broker has to be someone whom you trust. In introducing the potential partner, the broker puts her or his own reputation in jeopardy. If the person the broker introduces you to fails to live up to the recommendation, the broker loses reputation not just with you but with your entire network. Thus, brokering places a high responsibility on brokers, motivating them to provide trustworthy connections.

The East Asian cultural norm to communicate indirectly, especially when the information is negative, complicates the brokering process.[1] An interviewee from Japan explained:

The recommender generally avoids making negative recommenda-tions, so we have to observe the way the recommender recommends these (people). It's not direct. You know, the communication among Japanese people is highly implicit. (118, Japan)

When we asked how this Japanese manager knew when an indirect recommendation was negative, he told us, *We observe the genuine context inside recommendation, the gestures, tone of voice* (118, Japan), but he admitted that interpreting a broker's recommendation is not always easy and sometimes mistakes happen. In one case, his company only realized that a broker had been trying to signal that a potential partner was not a good fit after spending considerable time with the partner, wasting time and money. We note that his criticism was not of the broker for being indirect, but of his own company for not reading the indirect signals correctly.

Another interviewee, from China, described the challenge of signaling negative information indirectly from the perspective of being the broker.

Sometimes we are asked about some partners we have worked with before. I know this company is not really trustworthy, but I will not try to expose that person in public in order to keep a kind of normal or friendly atmosphere for the introduction. But in my mind, I know that this company is not trustworthy. Thus (when asked about) the people representing this company, I will try to put a question mark on their performance. (189, China)

East Asian managers rely heavily on brokering but, perhaps para-doxically, they also have to expend considerable effort interpreting the broker's recommendation. Because East Asians are used to a culture in which communication is indirect, they know to pay close attention to contextual cues when a broker is making an introduction. Failing to do so can be costly.

At the same time, relying on a broker for evidence that a potential partner is trustworthy is efficient in many ways. A brokered introduction can save a lot of time.

> *Japanese people tend to be doubtful when facing a new party so we like to get a good credential from a highly rated other party. In order to proceed with new business and a new partnership, the person in charge has to gather as much information as possible for the internal approval process. A good introduction from trusted party can be very useful for me to proceed with the process.* (118, Japan)

Due Diligence Is Also Key

Whether East Asians arrange a brokered introduction or not, they are likely to engage in some level of due diligence, particularly concerning the reputation of the company they are considering partnering with and the representative of the company they would be interacting with.

- *(If a) company is big enough or has potential to do enough business with us, that's the first criteria.* (130, Korea)
- *The client is a Fortune 500 company, so it's definitely trustable. They would not question the credibility of that company.* (103, China)
- *If that company has a good reputation, good brand, probably we will have a tendency to want to go with them.* (185, Hong Kong)
- *It depends on background, if you're a famous company, people know your background, they would trust.* (161, China)
- *If a company's name is known, in general they would trust.* (104, Japan)

The reputation of the person representing the company is also important, although not as important as the reputation of the company itself.

- *You do a lot of checking as a background before you meet the person.* (111, Thailand)
- *Before I meet a person it will be just get as much knowledge as possible about the person ... and after based on what he presents to me during the first encounter ... I would further validate with another round of due diligence.* (184, Singapore)
- *In order to trust, we have to know the people first rather than the business, so that means we need to know their background, including the ages and school relations.* (134, Korea)
- *Of course, the reputation of the individual is really important but the reputation of the group is more important than just the individual reputation. So for example, if someone is from LG or Samsung then it's easier for us to trust him. Someone graduated from Harvard and working for the small company – that is not what we prefer.* (134, Korea)

Interviewees also described the fiduciary element of due diligence.

- *I will also ask our legal people to check their lawsuit history, commercial registration, tax payment, records, all those kind of thing.* (192, China)
- *My company has a due diligence process to follow: who are shareholders, what are their finances, has there been any scandals. This mostly you can do online. Then meet with key person(s) making decisions; learning their mindset, view of the industry; why looking at opportunity with us; how manage own company; what are their goals moving forward.* (111, Thailand)

Finally, due diligence may be used to investigate competence.

- *We make sure what they have done, achievements.* (118, Japan)
- *People will ask people, do you know this person, how is this person? Whether this person will actually see through things or if this person's really just a talker?* (143, Singapore)

- *People they really focus on the benefits from deal. And they are looking for a good reputation on their capabilities, on their deliverables.* (176, China)
- *Most businesses rely on all sorts of (investigations) on the potential partner that they are going to work with. So, a lot of them might out-source this kind of cost to a third party to help them reference check.* (174, Hong Kong)

Meet in Person to Assess Competence

After passing the hurdles of proving one's reputation and competence via information gathered indirectly in brokering and due diligence, the next key action in the trust development process in East Asia is organizing in-person business meetings.

- *Prefer first meeting to be face to face in office environment.* (188, Indonesia)
- *Prefer to get an interview in the office.* (189, China)
- *It would be in more of a business setting.* (185, Hong Kong)

The purpose of these in-person meetings is to test (again) for competence. *It's not like testing I trust you, but testing if you can do it* (103, China). Why this focus on testing competence in person? As mentioned previously, East Asian cultures are indirect communication cultures.[2] As the quotes suggest, in this culture, it is difficult to say explicitly, "No, we cannot do that." At the same time, East Asian managers explained that there is a tendency for embellishment. It is almost as though the embellishment is an indirect signal of a lack of competence. The driving force for meeting in person, then, is to sort out what a potential partner truly can and cannot do.

- *Chinese exaggerate so have to check out yourself; focus on their capabilities.* (176, China)
- *Sometimes people tell the things they cannot do. It's a big mistake and you lose trust completely. If you are in the industry, you know what's realistic and what's not.* (186, Japan)
- *(I would be concerned) when he express about the company, like our company has future revenue reaching a certain amount, but based on my research, those things are not really realistic.* (129, Korea)

East Asians want to know what a potential partner is truly capable of doing as opposed to embellishments about their capabilities. To pass the competency test, East Asians want facts and data, not rhetoric.

- *(See if) they can provide the information we want to know.* (158, China)
- *(Ask them) have they done a project like this before, how many people they try to assign, what type of professionals they have.* (118, Japan)
- *When they talk about their facts, we understand what we need, so if you talk about something that is even a little bit exaggerating, it would discount the trust we have from them.* (185, Hong Kong)
- *We would ask some questions that would check honesty and maybe authenticity.* (111, Thailand)
- *I don't feel comfortable if the people are trying to go around in circles instead of directly answering the questions. Then I know that he does not know the answer, but he's trying to play some tricks.* (189, China)

This focus on facts and data to judge competence is at least partially due to the difficulty East Asians have in saying "no" directly. Understanding indirect East Asian communication requires inferring meaning from the context of what is being said, as opposed to the literal meaning of the words being used.[3] A deep dive into why

East Asia is an indirect communication culture goes beyond the pur-
view of this book.[4] However, it might be useful here to recall the example in chapter 2 of different greeting behaviors. Communication,
like greetings, is a type of social interaction. And, as we discussed in
chapter 2, different cultures address the same problem of social interaction differently. Indirect communication is not necessarily a worse
or a better mode of communication than direct communication – it
is just different.

Of course, East Asians are well aware that communication in their
culture is indirect. We see this in the quotes above that describe how
managers asked for specific information to test for competence, and
in how they did their due diligence to help interpret the context of
the answers they received. This information, meant to reveal competence, ultimately serves as a good indicator of whether a deal will get
done. *But if there's no real deal on the table. I mean, there will be all
these conversations and stuff and then like it just can't move forward*
(143, Singapore).

Goodwill Building and Adherence to Cultural Norms

Once East Asian managers are confident that the potential partner is
competent, they might engage in goodwill building to assess adherence to cultural norms. A partner who does not adhere to cultural
norms might prove sooner or later to be an embarrassment. Such a
partner could also prove difficult to support if called on for a brokered
introduction.

- *So once I understand their key ideas, we are going out for drinks to
  talk about business.* (129, Korea)
- *Setting business dinner after successive or important meetings is fairly
  typical in Japan. On the other hand, before important meetings, we*

don't usually set informal opportunity to communicate. ... People are
usually afraid of imperiling good atmosphere or good relationship.
(118, Japan)

In East Asia goodwill building, which on the surface appears to be
a social celebration of the new relationship, nevertheless has an element of assessment. A major purpose of goodwill building in East Asia
is to assess potential partners in social situations, some of which may
be designed deliberately to test how the partner might act in a difficult
encounter. Evidence that potential partners adhere to social norms in
these goodwill-building social interactions provides reassurance that
their behaviors will not humiliate or shame the relationship.

- *It's all about manners. The person must know the Korean culture. We*
  don't really expect you to drink that bottom shot, but at least you take
  it. We like to see how you act, how you react. (130, Korea)
- *If the people are showing that they know like which seat to sit in the*
  taxi, which chair to sit in the long table, they are giving a message that
  I know the norms and I am a person who is trying to adopt that norm.
  (104, Japan)

Failure to adhere to social norms or failure to show respect for hierarchy can be costly in East Asia. The following story, relayed by a Japanese
interviewee, illustrates such consequences. In Japan (as in many other
places), consulting firms sometimes enter competitions to get new business, during which they make a presentation to the potential client. Sometimes they win the business and sometimes not. This story explains why
our interviewee's company lost one such competition. He found out by
asking a counterpart at the potential client's office why his firm had lost.

He told me that the content was really good, but because the num-
ber of the people we brought to the presentation and their rank was

lower than what our competitors brought to their presentation, the decision maker thought my firm was not showing effort and not committed enough to this project. (104, Japan)

The example above was not the only one emphasizing the need to show respect for hierarchy in East Asia. Several interviewees also mentioned the importance of paying attention to hierarchy.

- *Most of the Asian countries have a highly hierarchical social system, so for example, the older people have more power than younger people. So age is very important.* (134, Korea)
- *The second level in terms of research would be how senior is this person? Then if we are asking for a meeting, obviously you need to match the level.* (143, Singapore)

Goodwill building also helps East Asians develop trust with potential partners.

- *If we have a good conversation during dining, that will help you gain trust and help you to build a relationship with the person.* (185, Hong Kong)
- *Through the conversation, you will get the sense whether this kind of person is someone that is in line with you.* (174, Hong Kong)
- *It's really that people see things in the same way, people handle things in the same way. Then you are feeling that this is a person that you can work with.* (189, China)
- *Those who are proud of themselves and then exaggerate. Such kind of people we treat not trusting.* (165, Japan)

Three conclusions about the decision to trust stand out from our East Asian interviews. First, the decision to trust occurs in stages. Stage one establishes reputation; stage two, competence; and stage three, adherence to social norms. Second, in deciding to trust, people rely heavily on the opinions of others, but drawing conclusions from implicit communication is challenging even to East Asians who are accustomed to indirect speech. Third, East Asians use of in-person testing and goodwill building focuses on business relationships more than personal relationships.

Cultural Explanation: High-Trust, Homogenous, Tight Culture

In high-trust, homogeneous, tight cultures such as in East Asia, social norms and monitoring and sanctioning of deviations from normative behavior support high levels of trust. The working assumption is that people are trustworthy, not just because the cultural norm is high trust but because of the tight culture. In tight cultures, people are careful to build and to maintain good reputations. The result is that it is relatively easy to acquire reputational information about the trustworthiness of a potential partner via due diligence and brokering. The challenge in deciding to trust a potential partner in East Asian culture is determining whether the potential partner actually has the competence to deliver the project. This challenge is made more difficult because of the norm of indirect communication, the reluctance to say, "No, we can't do that." To work around indirect communication, East Asian managers described testing for competence during in-person meetings, presentations, and site visits. One might think that reputation and competence would be tightly coupled. However, circumstances change. A broker may have assured a potential partner, "She did a great job for me: quality performance, on-time delivery, easy to work with" but similar performance may not be possible under the partner's constraints.

High trust and cultural tightness explain the key actions East Asians take to decide to trust and why the primary CORR standard they rely on is competence. The World Values Survey data, first presented in chapter 2, show that East Asian cultures are high-trust cultures. However, high trust in East Asia is limited to people East Asians know or have connections to. In East Asia, strangers are less likely to benefit from the assumption of trust than family, friends, co-workers, or even people from your high school or hometown. This is because having a connection means that you and the other person are part of the same social monitoring and sanctioning system.

- *I normally trust people I work with.* (186, Japan)
- *People mostly trust people they know.* (192, China)
- *Normally we trust our friends much more than the newcomer.* (189, China)

Strangers in East Asia can overcome the trust gap by identifying a common connection perhaps via a common experience. A Chinese interviewee gave us this example: a broker introduced him to a potential new customer. Upon meeting, they discovered they grew up in the same city. He explained,

> *We got talking about our early childhood, our middle school, the best food in our city. So those sort of very specific things, and because this is a person who shares the same experiences and memories as you do, is an echo from yourself, you're feeling that this really good personal contact can easily result in the good business output.* (189, China)

The homogeneity of tight East Asian cultures aids people in their decisions about whether to trust strangers. In the example above, the potential partners learned that they had common origins and common experiences. They shared tight-culture norms, which reassured them that trust was justified. To recap, tight cultures have many social norms governing everyday activities. These norms are strong because of social monitoring and sanctioning of deviations from normatively acceptable behavior. Most East Asian nations (e.g., Korea, Japan, and China) are ethnically homogeneous but even the most ethnically heterogeneous East Asian nation, Singapore, uses a single set of social norms to control social interaction.

- *We have a lot of social norms actually.* (129, Korea)
- *When somebody breaks the norm, usually people will be blamed. Either someone will be expelled from the group or stamped as a black sheep.* (111, Thailand)
- *Ignoring them* (social norms) *may cause breaking a relationship with business partners or friends or family.* (118, Japan)
- *Singapore really (is) a city of immigrants, but at the same time because it's so multicultural, there are very strong social norms that I would say govern the way you interact to make sure that you keep the peace.* (143, Singapore)

This cultural combination of high trust and tight culture generates confidence in East Asia that people can predict trustworthy behavior of even an unknown person so long as the other person has a reputation to uphold socially, but especially if the introduction is brokered or they share a common background. Trust of people you work with generates confidence in positive information gathered via due diligence and brokering. A positive reputation in a tight culture generates expectations that others will adhere to social norms and act in a trustworthy fashion. Cultural tightness implies that people feel the subjective weight of others' expectations and know that their behavior will be sanctioned if they violate social norms. This is certainly why East Asians placed a lot of weight on brokered introductions.

Cultural tightness also manifested in the characteristically disciplined, systematic, and efficient manner East Asian managers described as the process of deciding to trust. They moved systematically through the key actions for gathering information to make the trust decision: the initial emphasis on brokering; then the focus on competence during testing; and, once competence was established, the assessment of the potential partner's commitment to cultural norms in goodwill building.

Cultural tightness, with its characteristic strict adherence to social norms, also explains East Asians' response to the challenge of assessing competence when norms for communication are indirect. An East Asian broker would be unlikely to violate the tight social norm of indirect communication by saying explicitly, "No, I cannot recommend that company or that person." Such a direct statement could cause the broker both embarrassment and loss of reputation. Instead, brokers might hedge their enthusiasm about making a connection or suggest checking out some of the prior projects that the potential partner had been involved in. In tight East Asian cultures, indirect communication gets the message across without any explicit statement of competence and thus no violation of the social norm of indirect communication.

Although some countries in East Asia are culturally tighter than others, in general, the region is marked by tightness and homogeneity. Such an environment helps explain why it is so important to have a good reputation in this region. For example, earning a good reputation in business or putting together an impressive educational background (by, say, working hard to be admitted to top schools) requires significant effort and significant investment in adherence to cultural norms. It would be costly to engage in actions that would compromise such an investment of resources. Thus, a partner with a good background is strongly motivated to maintain that good reputation and is likely to be considered trustworthy.

Advice on Developing New Business Relationships in East Asia

If you are from a culture in the East Asian region, you are likely to be familiar with what we've learned about the process of developing trust in new business relationships in that region. The cultural explanation of this process may be new to you and keeping in mind that East Asian cultures are typically tight, ethnically homogeneous, and high trust may be helpful to you and to others not from this region in searching for and deciding to trust in this region. Based on our research, we offer several recommendations to help build trusting relationships with potential partners in East Asia.

- Make a concerted effort to get an introduction. Brokering is very important in East Asia.
- Be sure to demonstrate credentials, facts, achievements, and any other reputational information early on in interactions. Answer questions by providing examples, prototypes, and prior work.
- Be aware that communication is indirect in East Asia. This means that you must pay attention to context and subtext to gain a full and accurate understanding. A lot goes unsaid and what goes unsaid may be as important as what is said.
- The group or company's reputation is more important than an individual's reputation. Recognize that although your individual education and achievements do matter, the group (institution, organization) that you represent matters more.
- Try to meet face to face.
- Don't expect social gatherings to happen until the new business relationship is in place.
- Demonstrate respect for social hierarchy and seniors. This means bringing the correct person of rank to meetings and even showing you know your own social status by where you sit in meetings.

Moving on to High-Trust, Loose Culture

A high-trust, tight culture makes it relatively easy for people to rely on brokered introductions and reputation. However, as we will see in the next chapter, high-trust, loose cultures do not rely on brokered introductions and reputation to the same degree as a high-trust, tight cultures. Loose cultures, as we saw in the chapter on Latin America, place a lot of responsibility on the person deciding to trust, relative to those making introductions or recommendations. With high-trust, loose cultures, the assumption is the other person is trustworthy, but the process is focused on testing.

CHAPTER 6

The West – Be Open to Sharing Information

- *We operate under the principle everyone can be trusted until proven otherwise.* (142, US)
- *We are quite flexible with those (cultural) norms.* (162, Finland)

In the West, people generally assume others are trustworthy but, to avoid being taken advantage of, they are likely to test that assumption. The purpose of the test is to see how open and forthcoming the person to be trusted is. The test is not about personal self-disclosure but about willingness to share information that will facilitate a potential business relationship.

- *In the US we push the business side and trust the human side will follow.* (138, US)
- *Kind of the concept of business is business and family is family. I think in the US context, there's probably a little bit of separation, more separation there than you would see in other parts of the world.* (106, US)
- *Sometimes you also like people or you like your suppliers, but you have to separate the personal relationship from the work.* (172, Italy)

- *It doesn't matter how nice the people are or how much you like them, if they don't have enough business, they don't have enough business.* (123, US)

In the West, managers placed a priority on the business relationship and assumed that if a personal relationship developed, it would follow from the business relationship. Contrast this approach to what we learned about deciding to trust in Latin America, where the focus was on developing rapport and the assumption was that if the personal relationship developed, the business relationship would follow.

The Openness Test

Western culture managers used all four key actions (due diligence, brokering, goodwill building, and testing) to generate information relevant to the decision to trust but they relied primarily on testing. The assumption that people generally are trustworthy resulted in Western culture managers moving quickly to in-person meetings in which they tested their assumption of the potential partner's trustworthiness and signaled their own trustworthiness by engaging the potential partner in frank and reciprocal sharing of information relevant to the business relationship.

- *Test their openness, willingness to share.* (106, US)
- *Are they open in demeanor; do they answer questions thoroughly?* (108, US)
- *See if person is forthcoming; ask a question you know the answer to.* (142, US)
- *You don't want to play games, but at the same time, for example, there's a lot of public information out there. So hey, I found this on the internet. I saw this press release. Help me understand more about that.* (126, US)

- *You tend to do the similar question with two different angles in order to understand that you get a similar answer, so this is a typical way to understand if you have someone that is hiding something or is trying to paint reality in a different way.* (141, Italy)
- *Does the party reciprocate your information? Trust builds trust, so you certainly want to start out on the right foot and look for information that you could exchange that would build some level of trust.* (150, US)
- *I think you build trust by sharing information. If you have someone who's pretty open to you, who shares a lot of information, I think it feels like he's trusting in you, so you trust in him. If it's only give, and there's no take, or if there's only a take from his side and no give, then it's not a fair dialog.* (127, Germany)

These quotes illustrate how, in the West, the process of deciding to trust is a two-way street with regard to openness. Managers were willing to share information about the business model with the potential partner and they expected the potential partner to share in return. Reciprocal information sharing minimizes risk and builds trust,[1] thereby removing potential roadblocks to new business relationships.

One US interviewee told us about how open information sharing allowed him to build trust with a potential partner who was not the final decision maker in his company, but someone who could connect him with key decision makers.

Who do you trust? Who do you go to, who do you develop a relationship with, and who is the real decision maker? Over about eight months, I developed a relationship with the main corporate buyer. We found common ground on a personal level, as we had a similar philosophy in terms of trying to do the best for our companies. (We agreed) the best way to do that was through open communication. And from there we helped each other. He made suggestions about *making connections with (decision makers). At the end of the day, we ended up going from a zero dollar relationship on a particular product line to a $4 million relationship.* (142, US)

Note in this quote that what established "common ground on a personal level" was finding out that both managers shared a philosophy about doing business. How different this is from Latin America, where establishing common ground on a personal level was extremely important but the common ground was more related to personal philosophy of life than a philosophy of business.

Another interviewee told us a story about how her organization ultimately built trust all the way down through the partner's organization but doing so first required gaining the trust of a specific gatekeeper who was initially closed off.

They had a person who was a gatekeeper. She was empowered with decision-making ability, but she had been very, very closed off. I suggested that we do a full executive meeting with both companies. That's not something you usually see within our space. Our CEO doesn't normally present, I mean, I can count on my hands the times that he's met with a client directly over the past few years. He gave some short points on who we are, what we're doing, and what we're driving at. She was able to see her CEO buy into us as a company. That took down all of those barriers that she had put up previously. It allowed her to move forward and ask collaborative questions, in a "how do we partner" sort of way instead of an "I'm looking for something" wrong kind of way, which is what we were running into before. (123, US)

These two stories highlight the value of openly sharing information so that both partners understand that they share a common vision for their potential business. In the first story, this led to valuable introductions that built business. In the second story, this led to a gatekeeper's pivot from defensive to collaborative behavior and new business. Western culture researchers have described this process of building trust to generate cooperation "as an intricate dance that spirals over time and is fundamentally affected by partners' initial moves."[2] Our interviewees' stories illustrate how this process works in practice in Western culture.

Business versus Personal Relationships

To be sure, Western culture managers are not blind to the conduct of people they are meeting and interacting with. They prefer eye contact, a firm handshake, and expressions of warmth and respect. One interviewee called this "personal presence"; we would call it professionalism. A lack of professionalism makes it more difficult to trust, as the quotes below indicate, but may not necessarily preclude a business relationship.

- *You can carry yourself in a way that is warm and welcoming and that may cause the other side ... to trust you more. Or you could carry yourself as kind of rigid and cold and you may generate a response that's less trustworthy. (122, US)*
- *If someone is not looking you in the eye or doesn't shake your hand, it can make them seem not genuine. (193, US)*
- *Do they have just general good business etiquette? I've been to places – especially on the West Coast – you go there, sit down. You know these kids in hoodies and stained t-shirts come in and ask for millions of dollars. Again, maybe I'm old-fashioned, but to me, I'm like, am I going to trust this person? (126, US)*

Westerners' focus on building a business relationship – as opposed to a personal relationship – was also evident in how our interviewees talked about goodwill building, which they used as a prelude to discussing the business relationship. They told us that they liked to know something personal about their potential partners in hopes of discovering common interests or experiences, but the time they spent goodwill building was minimal.

- *Schmoozing doesn't build trust, expertise does ... move quickly beyond the icebreakers.* (150, US)
- *Of course, it's not totally no small talk, but it's like an introduction and maybe discussing something which is a common interest, like I would say ice hockey, but then it's an introduction about the companies and people and what they do and so on.* (162, Finland)

One interviewee told us that he turns on the local news when traveling to be able to start a business meeting with something of local interest to talk about but then quickly proceeds to the business:

> *I travel a lot for business. And if I have to spend the night, the first thing I do is put on the local news, so I know what's going on. When I go into a business meeting with people I'm meeting for the first time, I can start with "I hear that you guys got a lot of rain in the past couple of weeks. How are you doing with that?" or "Your sports team is doing great." I think that's definitely something done in US culture to start a meeting, and that will help me understand how open the other side is going to be, how engaging they're going to be. So, I say start with that, but I don't know. Within US culture, I don't think it necessarily goes on for a half an hour. I think it's relatively short, a few sentences, and then move into the business.* (108, US)

The above quotes highlight how Western managers use small talk or "schmoozing" strategically to ease into opening the business meeting. This is consistent with other research that shows that a little schmoozing builds rapport in Western contexts.[3]

Due Diligence and Brokered Introductions

Western managers engaged in due diligence, but there was no consistent timing for it. Some interviewees said they used due diligence before meeting face to face.

- *So that's probably something I would do before walking into a meeting if I knew who my counterparty was.* (108, US)
- *You start to do some pre-check, either to web or to a business connection, to see if your current business partners dealt with the company or with the person in the past ... and you try to get at least a couple of this kind of references, and these help a lot.* (141, Italy)

Others described due diligence as follow-up after it was clear that there was a potential for a work relationship:

Once I have established some position (the other party is interested in his product) and they have asked, "Do you have any reference whom we can contact?" I have got information afterwards that the guy has got a phone call and there has been a discussion, about what kind of person I am and so on. (162, Finland)

Still others just used due diligence if, after meeting in person, they did not feel entirely comfortable with the potential partner: *Only after you find things that are quite questionable, that's where you normally start to look for more and more detail to references* (141, Italy).

Western managers tended to be cautious in their use of reputational information gleaned from due diligence or brokering.

- *To be completely honest, I'm very careful with that (seeking references), because I've done that before with hiring people with really positive recommendations from people that I really trust. And then, it ended up not to be a great hire. I was way too trusting of the person that gave me the recommendation.* (193, US)

- *No, I don't think it's necessary (to seek references), quite frankly. You need each other. And then you get to know each other. In my experience, you can spend like three weeks trying to find out a little bit of information, which you get in a meeting in five minutes. I would probably feel a bit uneasy if I find out that before someone meets me they had already done a background check on me.* (127, Germany)

- *If a person has a bad reputation, you try to avoid that person, but I think there's always enough curiosity in proving people wrong sometimes. "Hey, I heard that," but then people want to find out for themselves.* (105, Switzerland)

Western managers recognized the value of introductions, but they did not treat introductions as brokered in the way East Asian managers did. In the quote that follows, the speaker clearly indicates confidence in the third-party matchmaker, but there is no sense that it would be the third party's fault if the match isn't good. *Because the matchmaker, so to speak, knows something about Party A and something about Party B. And again, my assumption is that person is not going to put two dogs that want to fight in the same pen* (126, US). Other Western managers were wary of the motivations of such a matchmaker.

- *You've got somebody that you do really well with and they're trying to introduce you to someone else. And the question you always ask is, what's in it for the person introducing me? I pay attention to where the motives are. Are they going to need something for this? What is it?* (123, US)

- *In this culture, people want to understand the broker's position, how they are incentivized, and then decide on trustworthiness from there.* (122, US)

- *Myself and my friends try to build the trust on their own with the counterpart, not to trust somebody else who introduced us.* (107, Poland)

These quotes highlight how Western managers primarily relied on their own individual assessment of a potential partner as opposed to placing significant weight on what others said about the partner. Western managers preferred to depend on the information they gathered themselves when meeting in person and testing for openness.

Cultural Explanation: High-Trust, Loose Culture

High trust and looseness generate a unique Western culture process of deciding to trust. High trust means that people assume others are trustworthy, but cultural looseness means there is a lot of variability in how strongly people adhere to social norms. In such a context, managers in Western culture clearly understood that not everyone was trustworthy. They actively tested the validity of their assumption of trust: *Trust but verify; people are not on the watch for distrust, but don't ignore signs either* (150, US). They also relied much more heavily on their own opinions than on those of references, a decision-making process characteristic of people in loose cultures.[4]

Managers we interviewed confirmed that their cultures were relatively high trust and loose, as represented by exhibits 2.3 and 2.4 in chapter 2. Trust was high across the region:

- *Italian people are quite open. We are not culturally very suspicious, and we tend to believe that people are trustworthy.* (141, Italy)
- *We operate under the principle everyone can be trusted until proven otherwise.* (142, US)
- *Finnish people, they believe very much in trust and that once people promise something, it's some kind of honor that it will be done as*

*promised, so it's quite much based on trust and people are very honest
to each other.* (162, Finland)

Similarly, managers described their Western cultures as loose with
respect to the strength of social norms.[5]

- *In the business world there's a way of behaving, but it's pretty laid back.*
  (105, Switzerland)
- *The north of Italy is much more European, so people tend to be less
  social norm-oriented. From Rome to the south, there are lots of
  cultural norms that tend to influence peoples' way of living and also
  people's way of thinking.* (141, Italy)
- *It's not as rigid as some other areas that I do business in. But I do think
  there still are norms.* (193, US)
- *Most of the time I never notice it (cultural norms) until somebody
  breaks a social norm. And then you realize wait, that's not how it's
  done. It's done like this.* (123, US)

Western and East Asian cultures share high trust, but what makes
high trust a reasonable assumption in these two regions is not the same.
Tight culture, that is, social monitoring and sanctioning of deviance,
keeps trust high in East Asia. Although loose cultures have social norms,
they also tolerate behavioral flexibility.[6] What then keeps trust high in
the West?

In chapter 2 we reported that adherence to the Protestant ethic and
institutional structures constrain the corrupt tendencies of political
and business leaders and support the high trust that is characteristic
of Western cultures. At the same time, Western cultures are relatively
loose and tolerant of behavioral flexibility around adherence to social
norms. As a result, there is more uncertainty about whether others can
be trusted in high-trust, loose Western than in high-trust, tight East
Asian cultures.

Western culture managers engaged in their own brand of in-person testing to search for information to test their assumption that the potential partner was trustworthy. In loose cultures, it is normative to challenge standard procedures, ignore constraints, and search for your own answers.[7] We found Western culture managers were much more likely to rely on their own opinions than on the opinions of others. For example, some Western culture managers checked references before a meeting with a potential partner. Others waited until they were sure there was potential for a business relationship. Still others did little or no checking, relying on their own judgment, and more than one manager told us he was willing to set aside negative information about the potential partner uncovered in due diligence and see for himself.

Loose Western culture afforded managers the liberty to rely on their own personal assessment of the potential partner's trustworthiness. High trust allowed them to move directly into substantive discussion about a potential business relationship. There, after minimal small talk – which in other regions would likely occur in a social setting, whereas in the West would likely take place in an office – Western managers tested their assumption of trust by evaluating how open the potential partner was in sharing and reciprocating information.

Advice on Developing Trust

If you are from a Western culture, you are likely to be familiar with what we've learned about the process of developing trust in new business relationships in this region. The cultural explanation of this process may be new to you and keeping in mind that this is a region of high trust and cultural looseness may help you and others not from this region in searching for and deciding to trust. Based on our research, we offer several recommendations to help build trusting relationships with potential partners in this region.

- Go into the relationship knowing that you are likely to be trusted initially and tested continually throughout your conversations.
- Be ready to share information. Answer questions as openly and thoroughly as possible. When asked about information you cannot share, explain why, and possibly under what conditions you could share the information.
- Require reciprocity of information sharing.
- Don't expect extensive time spent discussing personal matters. Small talk is likely to be short and sweet, about the weather, sports.
- Be professional and demonstrate good business etiquette (e.g., look the other person in eye, give a firm handshake, dress in a way that demonstrates the meeting is an important one).
- Anticipate that some potential partners will do extensive research on you before meeting but others will ask you for references after the meeting.

Moving on to Consider Regional Differences and Similarities

This chapter ends our in-depth discussion of searching for and deciding to trust in four different regions of the world. Although we have drawn some inter-regional comparisons in each chapter, the next chapter highlights regional similarities and differences in the process of deciding to trust.

CHAPTER 7

Similarities and Differences – Points of Contact between Regions

Some of my colleagues from certain societies, especially in the West, they come across as quite transactional. However, cultivating the relationship is quite important, even in the very beginning when you are visiting a potential partner, you just don't get into business right away. You need to talk to them, ask them how they're doing and how are their lives and how are their families. (136, Saudi Arabia)

The opening quote illustrates how differently managers from Western versus Middle Eastern cultures approach meeting with a potential partner. However, our Saudi Arabian interviewee might just as well have been commenting on the difference between East Asians and Latin Americans. As the regional chapters explain, in the West and in East Asia, when meeting, managers focus on the business relationship. In contrast, in Latin America and the Middle East/South Asia, when meeting, managers focus on assessing the personal relationship first, reasoning that without trust there is little point in exploring the possibility of a business relationship. This similarity links regions that otherwise treat the decision to trust rather differently. Another similarity, but one that also links regions differently, is the relative reliance on own opinions versus own and others' opinions of a potential partner's trustworthiness. This similarity distinguishes Latin America and the West – where the emphasis is on own opinions – from East Asia and the Middle East/South Asia, where managers rely heavily on the opinions of others, particularly at the beginning of the process of deciding to trust a potential partner.

We highlight these inter-regional similarities in this chapter because they provide valuable points of contact when people are interacting across cultures. We explain the origins of these similarities in trust and tightness-looseness. However, we caution that even though managers in two different regions may take similar approaches to the process of deciding to trust, their approaches may manifest in different ways. They may use the same key actions to search for different information. For example, relative to managers in Latin America and the Middle East/South Asia, managers in East Asia and the West get down to business much more quickly. Managers in East Asia and the West use testing at this stage of the decision process, but they are testing for different CORR standards: competence in East Asia versus openness in the West. Alternatively, managers in two different regions may take similar approaches to the process of deciding to trust but their approaches may manifest in their use of the different key actions. For example, managers in Latin America and the West rely heavily on their own opinions to decide to trust; managers in Latin America develop their opinions during goodwill building while managers in the West do so in testing. The upshot is that although similarities provide important points of intercultural contact, embedded in similarities are differences.

Exhibit 7.1 organizes the similarities and differences in the process of deciding to trust by levels of cultural trust and tightness-looseness. The cultural starting point of low versus high trust manifests in the difference between the focus on the personal relationship in Latin America and the Middle East/South Asia and the focus on the business relationship in East Asia and the West. The cultural starting point of tightness versus looseness manifests in the stronger reliance on others' opinions of potential partners' trustworthiness in East Asia and the Middle East/South Asia than in Latin America and the West. Cultural similarities in trust and tightness-looseness also provide insight into similarities and differences in the ways managers use key actions to seek the information they need to decide to trust.

EXHIBIT 7.1. *Similarities and differences by region.*

	Tight	Loose
High Trust	East Asian Cultures: Competency • Focus: work relationship • Rely on others' and own opinions • Seek reputation • Test for competence	Western Cultures: Openness • Focus: work relationship • Rely on own opinion • Test for openness
Low Trust	Middle Eastern/South Asian Cultures: Respect • Focus: personal relationship • Rely on others' and own opinions • Seek reputation • Assess for respect	Latin American Cultures: Rapport • Focus: personal relationship • Rely on own opinion • Assess for rapport

Cultural Caveat

Before we begin to discuss similarities and differences, it is useful to recall, as discussed in the introduction and in chapter 2, that no cultural description is absolute. There is always behavioral variability within a culture, and you can expect more variability within a loose than a tight culture. Still, understanding what is culturally normative (the cultural mean or central tendency) is useful because that understanding prepares you to anticipate how people are likely to act and to label and understand those actions as cultural.

There are two major benefits of understanding the cultural origins of the way people act, especially when such behavior might be offensive in your own culture or just personally annoying to you. The first benefit is seeing differences as cultural.[1] This comes with recognizing that the behavior that is offensive or annoying to you is perfectly normal in the other person's culture. The result of such knowledge is your understanding that it is not so easy for them to switch off behavior that is culturally normative and not so reasonable for you to think they should. The second benefit is creativity. All this cultural insight motivates search for a creative response that respects cultural differences and allows cultural differences to co-exist.[2] To be sure, the creative response may be easier coming from you, if you are from a loose culture, than from them, if they are from a tight culture. Behavioral flexibility is built into loose culture DNA.[3] People from tight cultures can be behaviorally flexible. In fact, many bicultural people bridge tight and loose cultures, but building that bicultural expertise takes some time.[4]

High-Trust Cultures: Similarities in Use of Testing

In East Asia and the West, people generally anticipate that others are trustworthy. Given an a priori reason to trust the potential partner, the assessment of the potential of a working relationship comes first and the personal assessment comes second.[5] To be sure, the East Asians' reason for trusting is different from that of Westerners, as is the major CORR standard they rely on when deciding to trust, but both East Asians and Westerners focus on testing the potential working relationship when first meeting in person.

When Westerners and East Asians first meet in person with a potential partner from within their respective cultures, their cultural environments provide a relatively sound, although different, reason for assuming trust. In East Asia, cultural tightness means people rely on others' good reputations. Recall from chapter 5 that most East Asian cultures are homogeneous and tight. In these cultures, norms are strong, adherence to norms is monitored, and deviation from norms is sanctioned. Building a good reputation in a tight culture takes commitment to social norms. People adhere because having a good reputation has significant social advantages, for example, the ease of entering new relationships. Jeopardizing a good reputation, on the other hand, has significant social costs: *Once people start bad mouthing, it all goes downhill* (143, Singapore). Opportunities to rebuild a reputation, once lost, are limited, and so people are unlikely to take reputational risks in the first place. Homogeneous tightness means that reputations generalize across situations in East Asia.

In the West, cultural looseness means that people interact daily in an environment influenced by two factors that likely contribute to relatively high levels of interpersonal trust. One is the nature of the institutional environment in Western nations. Western governments and businesses are regulated and relatively transparent. The press is free. Western cultural institutions are by no means without flaws but the nature of the institutional environment, particularly the relatively uncorrupted courts,[6] minimizes corruption. The second factor that affects interpersonal trust in the West is the pervasive influence of the Protestant ethic: do unto others as you would have others do unto you.[7] The high cultural level of trust means that a potential partner is likely to be trustworthy. Starting with this assumption, Westerners easily test trust by signaling their assumption of trustworthiness and monitoring whether it is reciprocated. *We operate under the principle everyone can be trusted until proven otherwise* (142, US).

Starting from the assumption that others are likely to be trustworthy, managers in East Asia and the West use their initial in-person meetings to assess whether a business relationship makes sense. What is similar about the process of deciding to trust in these two regions is that the evidence calling trust into question is most likely to surface during a discussion of what they are attempting to do together as business partners.

Testing in East Asian cultures is likely to be a more formal process than testing in Western cultures. In East Asia, testing often begins with presentations and site visits – all directed toward demonstrating competence. Recall norms for communication in East Asian cultures are indirect relative to the West. This means the conclusion that the potential partner is competent is based on a lot of attention to the sub-text and strong inference. By contrast, in the West, testing often begins by sharing a vision of what the future working relationship could be – open information sharing. When reciprocated, this approach leads to a trust-amplifying cycle, confirming the assumption of trust in the context of the nature of the future work relationship. *Does the party reciprocate your information? Trust builds trust, so you certainly want to start out on the right foot and look for information that you could exchange that would build some level of trust* (150, US). Of course, the signal can be ignored. Not everyone can be trusted even in a high-trust culture. Cultural loose-ness, however, provides Westerners with the behavioral flexibility to pivot and exit quickly if their vision of the future working relationship is not reciprocated.

East Asia and the West are also different in the timing and use of goodwill building. In East Asia, goodwill-building social events typi-cally occur after parties are confident of the business relationship. *Before important meetings, we don't usually set informal opportunity to commu-nicate. ... People are usually afraid of imperiling good atmosphere or good relationship* (118, Japan). Goodwill building is a way to celebrate and demonstrate commitment to the new business relationship. However, it is also a further opportunity for testing whether the potential partner adheres to social norms or is likely to be a social embarrassment. In the West, goodwill building is likely to be a brief exchange of social talk that precedes talk about the business relationship. Its purpose is to ease into the business talk. *Schmoozing doesn't build trust, expertise does ... move quickly beyond the icebreakers* (150, US). Finding common interests, identifying common experiences, or even demonstrating openness is a potential side benefit but not the main purpose of goodwill building when deciding to trust in Western cultures.

Although there are many cultural differences between East Asia and the West, the shared focus on the business relationship and engagement in testing are important points of contact. To take maximum advantage of these similarities, however, East Asian and Western culture managers need to recognize that although both are using testing, each is searching for information to evaluate a different CORR standard: competence in East Asia and openness in the West.

Low-Trust Cultures: The Relationship Comes First

In Latin America and the Middle East/South Asia, people do not anticipate that others are trustworthy. Trust is low in these cultures; people are wary. With few reliable reasons to trust a potential partner, the assessment of the person comes first and the potential for a business relationship a distant second. Although Latin Americans and Middle Easterners/South Asians may have somewhat different reasons for their low trust and different CORR standards for trust, both focus their initial in-person meetings on whether they can have a personal relationship. Both use goodwill building to do this.

The reason for low trust in the Middle East/South Asia and Latin America is not entirely the same. Cultural tightness-looseness provides an explanation. Cultural tightness in the Middle East/South Asia means that people can reasonably assume others within their own family, tribe, or ethnic group are trustworthy. The trouble is extending that assumption across the subcultures that pervade this region. Low trust in the Middle East/South Asia reflects a history of tribal, religious, and ethnic conflict.[8] It is culturally smart to be wary of outsiders and culturally risky to trust them, yet people in low-trust cultures need to work together across communities. They not only need to co-exist, but economic development means they also need to collaborate. Goodwill building provides an opportunity for people to assess whether cooperation across subcultures is possible. The presumption is that people who demonstrate that they respect cultural differences are trustworthy.

That a stranger is trustworthy is a low-probability prediction in Latin America made even less likely by cultural looseness.[9] Heterogeneous Latin American cultures lack the strong social norms that mean Middle Easterners and South Asians can trust with relative confidence within but not between the subcultures that make up their societies. As discussed in chapter 4, Latin Americans also lack the transparent and relatively uncorrupted government and economic institutions and exposure to the Protestant ethic that facilitate high trust in Western cultures. The story by a Latin American interviewee in chapter 4, that he didn't even trust his brother when selling his car, is a startling and likely extreme example of low trust in Latin American society.

Because it is difficult to predict who is and who is not trustworthy in these generally low-trust cultures, Latin Americans and Middle Easterners/South Asians engage in goodwill building to find out. They use goodwill building at the same time in the process of deciding to trust but their use of goodwill building varies in terms of purpose and formality.

When meeting a potential business partner in person for the first time in the Middle East/South Asia or Latin America, prepare to invest significant time in goodwill building. One interviewee from the Middle East/South Asia region explained that just being willing to invest the time is a signal of the CORR standard of respect that guides Middle Eastern/South Asian managers' decisions to trust: *When you go and visit a place sometimes they offer hospitality. It begins maybe with tea and conversation. The host realizes that I don't know the city and offers to take me out for some good places to eat. So, because he is committing time, I feel a kind of connection between us* (177, India). An interviewee from Latin

America explained that it is in social occasions that people let down their guard and show who they really are, which provides information to judge the CORR standard of rapport that guides Latin American managers' decisions to trust. He said, *When you're talking about your family ... even if you try very, very hard, you cannot hide yourself for the whole two hours. There will be like five minutes where you're going to show your true colors, right? That's what you want to see* (179, Chile).

Goodwill building may be more formal in the Middle East/South Asia region than Latin America. Interviewees in the Middle East/South Asia region use the term *hospitality* to describe goodwill building. Was the potential partner treated as an honored guest? Did the potential partner graciously accept the host's hospitality? In Latin America goodwill building might occur in the context of being invited to family occasions, for example, the host's son's weekend football match or the family's Sunday dinner. What is important to remember is that these social occasions, whether formal or informal, are not just occasions to get to know the potential partner but occasions to assess the potential partner against the culture's CORR standard for trust.

We discussed in chapter 4 why rapport is so important in Latin America, but it is respect that is prized in Middle Eastern and South Asian cultures. We proposed that this difference is due to the contrast between the moderately heterogeneous, loose Latin American cultures and the strongly heterogeneous, tight Middle Eastern and South Asian cultures. Differences in Latin America are not so starkly drawn and are thus potentially easier to bridge with shared values than differences in the Middle East/South Asia where the bridge is mutual respect of different values.

Although there are many cultural differences between Latin America and the Middle East/South Asia, an important point of contact is the shared focus on the personal relationship and engagement in goodwill building. To take maximum advantage of these similarities, however, Middle Eastern/South Asian and Latin American managers need to recognize that although both are using goodwill building, each is searching for information from goodwill building to evaluate a different CORR standard: rapport in Latin America and respect in the Middle East/South Asia.

Tight Cultures: Reliance on Own and Others' Opinions

East Asians, Middle Easterners, and South Asians all rely heavily on the opinions of others in the initial stage of deciding to trust. They follow standard procedures: collecting information via due diligence and seeking introductions via brokers whom they trust. They assume that the information that others provide is likely to be sound. Cultural tightness explains why people follow standard procedures in searching for and deciding to trust in these regions. Cultural tightness means that rules govern everyday life. Cultural tightness also justifies the assumption that reputational information is reliable. People in tight cultures who provide brokered introductions are careful not to jeopardize their own reputations by recommending people whom they do not trust. It is for this reason that brokered introductions carry significant weight in these regions.

However, brokers may be more difficult to identify in Middle Eastern/ South Asian cultures than in East Asian cultures. People who can broker across subculture boundaries in heterogeneous, tight Middle Eastern/ South Asian cultures may be in short supply because there may be few people who have contacts that cross subculture boundaries. In contrast, because East Asian cultures lack subculture boundaries, brokers may be relatively easy to identify.

Identifying a broker in East Asia may be easy but understanding that broker may be more difficult than understanding a broker in Middle Eastern/South Asian cultures. Norms of communication are more direct in Middle Eastern/South Asian than in East Asian cultures: *People don't keep secrets here, so they tell you everything* (115, Palestine). In East

Asia, recall the difficulty of understanding a less-than-enthusiastic broker: *The recommender generally avoids making negative recommendations, so we have to observe the way the recommender recommends these (people)* (118, Japan). Although managers in both regions rely on brokering, there is work in finding a broker in the Middle Eastern/South Asian cultures and in understanding the broker in East Asian cultures.

When a potential partner's reputation checks out via brokering and due diligence, managers in the Middle East/South Asia and East Asia want in-person meetings during which they can form their own opinions. However, Middle Easterners/South Asians and East Asians' key actions diverge and their different CORR standards for deciding to trust surface in this in-person stage of the process of deciding to trust. The Middle Easterners/South Asians gather information to judge respect via goodwill building. The East Asians gather information about competence via testing.

Managers in the Middle East/South Asia and East Asia have several points of contact in the initial stage of the process of deciding to trust. Managers from both regions recognize that a good reputation is hard won and highly valued. They also share the tight-culture penchant for systematically seeking reputational information via due diligence and brokered introductions. .

Loose Cultures: A Reliance on Own Opinions

The balance between reliance on own opinion versus own and others' opinions tips strongly toward reliance on own opinions in Latin American and Western cultures. People in Latin America versus the West have very different expectations of a potential partner's trustworthiness (Latin America, low trust; the West, high trust) but they share the loose-culture propensity to rely heavily on their own assessments to decide whether to trust. The relatively weak social norms that are characteristic of loose cultures mean that people can choose their behavior from among a range of normatively acceptable options. With so much behavioral variation in social interaction, people develop the behavioral capacity to assess others. They do not rely on social norms to predict others' behaviors; they rely on their own observations of what people do.

Behavioral flexibility in loose cultures means that people do not assume that reputational information provided by others generalizes across situations. Some of the managers we talked to learned this the hard way: *I was way too trusting of the person that gave me the recommendation* (193, US). *In business you don't know how a person can react in certain specific moments of his life* (181, Peru). Regardless of whether the culture is low or high trust, loose culture burdens the decision maker with the risk of deciding to trust a potential partner. This is the key point of contact between Latin American and Western cultures. In both regions, managers minimize risk by relying heavily on their own rather than others' opinions of their potential partners.

Although Latin American and Western culture managers' reliance on their own opinions is similar, their CORR standard for decision making and the key actions they engage in to search for information to make the decision to trust differ. Latin Americans assess rapport in what seems to Westerners lengthy goodwill building. Westerners test openness in business meetings. Managers from both regions share the assumption that reputational information provided by others may not generalize across situations. They also share the loose-culture tendency to rely on in-person information gathering.

Meeting in Person

Although different cultures generate different approaches to addressing the same problem of deciding to trust, people are social. They want to meet and get to know the people they may be working with. Although our research identifies many regional cultural differences in the process of deciding to trust, there is one important overarching similarity: everyone we talked to wanted to meet those with whom they would be doing business. When we conducted the interviews that provide the core evidence for this book, meeting face to face meant sitting together in person. What happens when a crisis, such as the COVID-19 pandemic, makes those in-person meetings no longer possible? In late fall 2020, we re-interviewed 21 managers from across our four regions (4–6 people per region) to learn how the difficulties associated with meeting in person affected the process of searching for and deciding to trust a potential business partner. In the next chapter, we describe how the pandemic affected their search for trust. In the subsequent chapter, we report their views of the how the process of searching for trust might change in a post-pandemic future.

CHAPTER 8

Searching for Trust during a Pandemic

Across cultures, the managers we interviewed before COVID-19 believed meeting in person offered the best opportunity for judging a potential partner against their culture's primary CORR trust standard. Wanting to know how the pandemic-related barriers to meeting in person were affecting managers' ability to decide to trust, we reconnected with 21 of our original interviewees in the fall of 2020. We asked them how the pandemic was affecting business development with new partners, and we asked what they thought the process of deciding to trust a potential new business partner would be like in the post-pandemic future.

They had a lot to say! Pandemic-related barriers to meeting in person were significantly limiting the development of new business relationships. Everyone was using video technology to get face to face with potential partners. However, face to face on the flat screen was not a satisfactory alternative to many who had money to spend but wanted the assurances of in-person meetings and site visits before deciding to trust. In this chapter, we describe regional differences in the effect of the pandemic on new business development and highlight the creative approaches managers in some regions were using to keep developing new business. The following chapter focuses on managers' views about the process of deciding to trust in the post-pandemic future.

Building Trust and New Business: Regional Differences

The pandemic affected building trust and new business relationships differently in different regions of the world. China, particularly, and East Asia, more generally, were outliers compared to the other regions. When we interviewed in the fall of 2020, travel within China was almost unrestricted; business, and the pursuit of new business relationships within China, was back to pre-pandemic normal. One interviewee explained, *The government simply extended the Chinese Spring Festival[1] into a much longer time. For most people, the COVID-19 Era was quite a long holiday. And then we got into the end of March, beginning of April (2020), and things started to become normal* (189, China). "Normal" meant travel for in-person meetings as well as business lunches or dinners. Business in other East Asian countries also largely went back to normal after the spring 2020 hiatus. *Our lockdown was short April-May, and because it was short, I could just postpone* (some business discussions) *including telling one party we were not going to work together* (111, Thailand).[2]

The experiences of managers in the Middle East/South Asia, Latin America, and the West were very different from those in China and East Asia. They continued trying to develop new business, but the consensus was that doing so during the pandemic was very difficult because they could not meet in person to assess risk and so decide to trust.

- *The place where you see the biggest difference is when you're trying to form new relationships, that's much more difficult. We are doing some of that, but with a much, much lower success rate than before COVID-19.* (123, US)
- *Getting deals from potential customers is way more difficult than with the old customers whom we know already, because you cannot have that in-person kind of interaction. We need to really have trusted*

partners because there are risks and if something fails costs are pretty high. We don't want to take any additional risks now. (162, Finland)

These quotes illustrate why the in-person part of the process of deciding to trust that we described in the regional chapters is so important in establishing new business relationships. The quotes also illustrate the potential consequences of not being able to meet in person to establish trust. Another interviewee, from the US, explained in detail how the lack of interpersonal interaction affected his ability to decide to trust.

How I determine someone is forthright and open and forthcoming with information is by generally sitting in front of them through a number of interactions where you can see the whole picture. You watch their body language. You watch their eyes; you feel the handshake. You have a chat and get to know them a little bit, not necessarily about business, but just about their family life, just like we did briefly at the beginning of this call. With the pandemic (video conferencing) *you have fewer visual sensory cues and fewer opportunities to develop that set of experiences from which to draw your conclusion. So each inter-action, you need to work harder to develop that connection because there are fewer interactions and they're not in person.* (142, US)

The problem of deciding to trust under these unprecedented circumstances was not limited to the West, which puts a high value on openness. Interviewees in the Middle East/South Asia, who face a low-trust environment and live in a culture that puts a high value on respect, bemoaned their inability to meet in person and frankly admitted it meant putting new business on hold.

• *You need to work really hard in order to gain the trust of your business partner and that needs a lot of communication, face to face. People decide if they feel comfortable with you during a meeting (in person). Do I want to work with this guy or not? COVID-19 has badly impacted the business. I'm not going to send my money to anybody that I don't know, and just wait for him to send me my products that I bought. I can't take (that) risk to make new business. (115, Palestine)*

- *(The pandemic) definitely has affected our ability to source and originate opportunities as well as to execute and manage the deals that we have. We have taken a quite a hit in the last nine months. A lot of potential partners have decided to take, you know, a wait-and-hold approach, a let's watch what's happening, kind of position. (136, Saudi Arabia)*

The experience was still different in Latin America. All our Latin American interviewees discussed how the pandemic at first caused business to pause, but faced with a need to generate revenue, business restarted, although with changes in how people approached new business opportunities.

People in Latin America always try to find a way to meet in person. At the beginning, we postponed decisions, let's meet in three months, hoping that it (the pandemic) would be finished. Nowadays, with it still going on, well you cannot stop your business. (183, Uruguay)

Another interviewee explained that with changing circumstances, old ways of doing business in Latin America were shifting.

I think that something very interesting has developed. I believe that this pandemic will leave a lot of benefits for the region, because we are evolving in the way we interact and in the way we are doing business, because we are all in a lot of need. (144, Bolivia)

We heard a similar theme talking to an interviewee from Brazil.

After COVID-19, face to face became challenging. So people found ways on keeping the spirit of being face to face, but using technology. But the principle of talking to someone (is the same). Trying to understand a little bit what this person brings to you and what kind of connection that you have with this person is still the key thing. (145, Brazil)

Our Bolivian interviewee thought that what he called the "beast" of culture, or the idea that you really need to get to know the other person, had lifted a bit.

And I think there is a deep understanding of the need of getting rid of having to know the other party too well before starting to do business. I think the barriers have gone down in terms of how much I need to know you personally. So it's like the beast, the cultural element (referring to getting to know the other party) is somehow present but has also lowered. (144, Bolivia)

What Has Changed?

The pandemic made it extremely difficult to develop new business relationships in many regions of the world. Two new themes emerged from our 2020 interviews: the challenge of meeting new business prospects and the challenge of not being able to meet in person to decide whether to trust a potential partner. One result was that interviewees reported establishing fewer new relationships; in place, they worked to double down on old relationships. Another result was that managers got creative and adapted, at least for the short term.

MEETING NEW PROSPECTS

Before COVID-19, meeting potential new business partners was relatively easy. Many "meet-ups" occurred at industry gatherings – the Consumer Electronics Show in Las Vegas, the MIPIM Real Estate Market in Cannes, the Berlin Fruit Logistica, and others. Other "meet-ups" followed from "cold" calls or "cold" emails. For example, "I am looking for someone to do ..., can we talk about what you could do for me?" ("Cold" here refers to calls or emails not based on prior introductions; the sender and the recipient do not formally know each other.) Although most large events were shuttered in the spring of 2020 and many people halted initiating new relationships directly, by late summer and fall of 2020 new approaches had emerged.

TRADE SHOWS

One of the best ways to contact potential new business partners pre-pandemic was trade shows and fairs that introduced new products, services, or opportunities. Interviewees lamented a lack of new contacts.

> So when it comes to the origination side. And I think the best example would be, I was supposed to be in Cannes in France for a real estate conference in March. We were counting on that conference to meet a lot of potential partners. And unfortunately, that got cancelled and it has halted and affected our origination efforts. (136, Saudi Arabia)

Trade shows and industry fairs promote mingling. As people wander through huge convention centers, pausing to chat at booths displaying new products, they might arrange a follow-up meeting or, at a minimum, leave a business card – an act to which they can refer in a follow-up call or email. As they wander around, they run into people they would like to meet, pause, introduce themselves, and perhaps suggest having a coffee or a drink, not so much to talk business as to identify common interests.

> The in-person fairs, you just meet people walking around. The big fairs, it's really overwhelming, but it's really amazing because even just walking through the halls, we see something even just the packaging, or something from a small potential client, and this is a great way to try it out and say hey, would you be interested ... (172, Italy)

In-person trade shows and fairs facilitate the informal interaction that our research shows is fundamental to developing new business relationships everywhere in the world. Putting these shows and fairs online, as began to occur in the second half of 2020, does get new products and opportunities out in front of people. However, at least as of this writing, organizers and programmers, despite some very creative uses of technology, have not been able to replicate the informal "meet-ups" that are the engine of effectiveness in promoting new business relationships in these settings. As our interviewee lamented about these online fairs: *You can talk to anybody from whatever part of the world 24-7. But because it's online, and because you have other things to do, the fair kind of becomes a third, fourth priority, just a way just to see how other competitors exhibit and not really a way to find new customers* (172, Italy).

COLD CALLING AND EMAIL

Especially in the West, before COVID-19, interviewees were comfortable cold calling and cold emailing. If they had an interesting business opportunity and they could get to the right person, they were confident they could get a hearing. The pandemic changed all that. When people are working from home and not in the office, what phone number do you call? In short, you don't. You send an email and try to set up an online call, which managers quickly realized was not so easy to achieve with someone with whom they had no relationship. When managers could set up a call, everyone's time was so tightly scheduled that there was no time for even the brief getting-to-know-you small talk that passed for goodwill building in the West. The pandemic put an end to spontaneous calls.

Whereas previously you know, it wouldn't be uncommon for me to pick up the phone and call my peer at a different company and say hey let's grab coffee, let's grab lunch. I don't have business to talk about, but let's just compare notes in the market. But, I don't have the ability to do that now, because every interaction is about a specific deal. If you don't have a need to be with someone, the baseline is to not be with people. (122, US)

So too, the efficacy of cold emails has declined or possibly even ended. Because of the economic downturn caused by the pandemic, many companies have been searching desperately for new business, using technology to scrape potential leads and sending blasts of emails. The problem with email is basic but challenging: getting the email read even if it gets to the right person.

Now, because we are in a crisis, new companies are offering services to us that they would not in normal times. We are passing on those. Of course, we try to be polite and reply, but sometimes there are so many emails and proposals waiting. I need to sort all of them out and understand which ones are interesting to me, and which ones I want to deal with and that's very challenging because I cannot get any interaction with those companies and I don't even have time to go through all of those offers I get. (162, Finland)

REFERENCES AND BROKERED INTRODUCTIONS

To get access to potential partners and keep their businesses alive, managers especially in the West and Latin America, who in pre–COVID-19 days did not rely heavily on introductions, were probing their networks to find people, friends, acquaintances, and prior business partners whom they hoped could make introductions for them.

- *People are very actively using their networks. Someone that I have had contact with before sends me an email or calls me and says there is a person in this business looking for an opportunity of making business with you and this person asked me if I could set up a 15–20 minute call, just to introduce yourselves and the interests that you might have in common.* (144, Bolivia)

- *There's no formula for this. You just have to seek out the people in your network who can be the most helpful to you and who are willing to be helpful. And I've identified three or four of those people. I'll approach them and say, "I need to meet with a certain person. Can you help make that introduction for me?"* (122, US)
- *The importance of the references went like skyrocket, because it's not easy to make connections with someone you don't know. People more and more ask for references. Because right now, we cannot do anonymous contacts with people. You have emailing and everything, but that's not enough.* (131, Turkey)

In East Asia, references and brokered introductions – which were central to the process of searching for trust prior to the pandemic – continued to be key actions to start the process of business development in that region. *So introductions are core, very bread and butter. It's not like a partner that you typically will find on LinkedIn* (143, Singapore).

Even though by the fall of 2020 East Asians were doing more business in person than were managers in other regions, they were also meeting a lot online. We were curious whether brokered introductions could be successful if conducted entirely online. Our interviewee described how this could be difficult. As we learned in chapter 5, East Asians tend to be exceedingly indirect when the message is negative and when the message is delivered online it is even more difficult to interpret: *You know, communication among Japanese people is highly implicit, so we observe the genuine context inside the recommendation from the other party. In order to see that we have to meet in person. Actually, it is quite difficult to navigate that in an online meeting* (118, Japan).

Meeting Face to Face though Seldom in Person

The pandemic drove business meetings online all over the world, but the effect was not uniform across regions. Business was mostly normal in China, where there were few domestic travel restrictions. Business was closer to normal in other parts of East Asia, where people were working from offices much of the time, although a reduction in non-domestic travel had particular implications for those working in Singapore and Hong Kong. In other regions, in-person meetings were limited. Recall the quote above from a US interviewee: *If you don't have a need to be with someone, the baseline is to not be with people* (122, US). Our interviewee from Turkey put it more bluntly: *It's not easy to come face to face anymore. And if people are willing to be face to face that means they're not really smart because he's not taking precautions and that actually lowers the trust. So it would also affect business. You know, nobody wants to work with a stupid person* (131, Turkey). Responding to restrictions to meeting in person, managers quickly gained experience and got creative about meeting online.

BENEFITS OF MEETING ONLINE

Managers were swift to point out the differences between meeting in person versus online and they definitely saw advantages of meeting online versus meeting in person. Compared to in-person meetings, managers told us online meetings were shorter, *A Zoom meeting seldom lasts for six hours, but if you go to visit someone, that meeting could last for six hours* (177, India). One Latin American interviewee noted that when meetings were online, people were on time, *Whereas when it's face to face, you know, you're 15 minutes late, and it's okay, no problem especially in Latin America. But online that doesn't happen. I think it's taught people to be more punctual* (119, Nicaragua). There was broad consensus that online meetings were more organized compared to pre-pandemic in-person meetings.

- *It's more structured than I mean just meeting over dinner and having a casual discussion.* (127, Germany)
- *And the convenience of online communication encouraged us to be very focused and that results in creativity and innovation.* (118, Japan)

An interviewee from Singapore described in detail how online meetings had led to new business:

> *Six months into COVID-19 we actually recruited a new partner.* (Online) *everybody is like focused; you have them for that hour or that half an hour. And everybody's paying attention with video on. Maybe it's taken a little bit more time than, if you're having a coffee and a few drinks, but the partners that we brought on have actually been really good partners who have really gotten our business.* (143, Singapore)

One frequently mentioned benefit of online meetings is the larger number of people who could attend compared to when meetings are in person and people needed to travel to attend. Managers noted benefits that went beyond obvious savings in time and travel costs, including an increased availability of senior management to drop in and signal commitment to projects, and efficiencies in execution of business arrangements because of the involvement of lower-level people.

- *There's a tendency to have more people involved, because there's almost no incremental cost.* (127, Germany)
- *If it requires traveling to close a deal in a country, maybe one or two persons will go, no more than that. And nowadays* (meaning meeting

online) *is also an advantage because they are having more meetings with more people in the company, so they can have a better overview what is going on in the company that before they didn't have.* (183, Uruguay)

- *If a person is visiting us, he gets to meet our team, but if I am visiting him, I get to meet his team, but they don't meet our team. We had a request and I suggested that we do video conferencing. We both had all the team members come in at the beginning. We just said hello and then we continued with two key people. That gave a little more comfort* (to team members on both sides), *where they know each other by name, and they shared phone numbers and then instead of calling me they can, for example, directly call a team member for smaller issues.* (177, India)

Another interviewee viewed online conversations as facilitating creativity and innovation: *Creativity and innovation can be easily encouraged through online communication because we can do that everywhere, anytime we want* (118, Japan). Another had exactly the opposite perspective. *From my point of view, creativity is more difficult. In face-to-face meetings, there might be some joking and some bit of crazy thinking about what could be the solutions, but it's more difficult to get to that crazy creative mode in the teleconference when you cannot see expressions and all of that stuff from other people* (162, Finland). Indeed, other interviewees also saw many downsides of meeting online.

DOWNSIDES OF MEETING ONLINE

The significant downside of meeting online versus in person was how it complicated the decision to trust. Just as online conventions and fairs interfered with the informal "meet-ups" where so much information was exchanged, online meetings eliminated many chances to get to know the other person informally, to judge them in informal settings, to pick up the stray but relevant fact in passing and build personal relationships – all essential elements of the trust process.

- *It is the things which you don't learn because everything is on the agenda. If you do an online meeting, you do not devote sufficient time to offline discussion, which gives you clues.* (127, Germany)
- *Because in the virtual space you have less opportunity to get to know the other person. The time is very limited. You don't start chatting about your family or how you grew up. I perceive that is much more difficult to talk about personal things in a virtual environment than going for lunch with someone where the barriers go up or come down after some 30 minutes, one hour of being together.* (144, Bolivia)
- *We were all listening and watching the video and all that but it there's still a preference for face to face. You've got* (referring to in-person meeting) *all the other side conversations that will happen after the meetings and stuff. That* (referring to side conversations) *is currently happening over WhatsApp, or iMessage and on phone calls. But it's just the quickie catching up in the taxi or something like that. It's those in-person moments that you build trust with the partner.* (143, Singapore)

Our interviewee from Uruguay talked about what some companies were doing to try to build personal connections even when interaction was online. *Some companies are having, let's call it after office meetings. Okay grab a coffee or glass of wine and let's have these non-business conversations in order to know a little bit more about each other. Because if we are going to be partners, I think it is a key that we can trust each other.* When we asked, "Do people actually get to know about the personal lives of others through those types of engagements?" the answer was, *This part is not easy, because it's not that you're sitting next to other person, and you have a one-to-one conversation, you are in a* (online) *meeting room with everyone. But, at least these kind of events give you some information that after you can refer to* (183, Uruguay).[3]

There was general agreement that it is better to have your video camera on than off when it comes to building relationships in virtual settings.

- *Very important to have the camera on when you have a meeting, because you want to see the person's face and their expressions when they talk. You want to see what the reaction is* (to what you are saying). *Face to face* (referring to in-person) *makes a big difference on building trust between the two parties. So, I think that's why* (video on) *is a prerequisite to helping build a trusting relationship.* (119, Nicaragua)
- *I try to use the video feature. And a lot of people don't want to turn the video camera on. That makes it a lot harder for me to develop relationships. And I know it's harder for other folks to develop a relationship with me.* (142, US)
- *We've replaced so much of face-to-face interaction with virtual interaction and video has become so much more prevalent than it was. It* (virtual interaction) *changes a little bit of the nuance and for me. One of the bigger changes is actually whether someone does video or not. When you are doing meetings, particularly when you have a group meeting and you have four or five people and someone chooses not to* (use video). *You start to go down the road of why would you have your video off when you're in this important setting? Either you're not paying attention, or you aren't prepared. So it changes the dynamic and how you feel about that person.* (123, US)
- *For me personally it's a huge difference whether you just talk on the phone without video like we are doing* (referring to the interview for this book).[4] *If your video is switched on I think you get a sense of the person. Everyone's at home right now. It's almost like having a private meeting. People are not dressed up and sometimes human things happen, kids walk in and these kind of things. It gives a personal touch which we wouldn't have if we meet in the office. I think it may be a bit easier because you still see me and either we connect or not.* (127, Germany)

- *If you're face to face* (referring to in-person), *talking, that's the best because then you see the gestures. You see the feelings, if a person is smiling or not. And so, I think we jumped to the second best thing* (referring to online video and audio). (131, Turkey)
- *I try to do as much over video as I can. Just because facial expressions, body language are so vital to picking up on the cues of what someone is communicating.* (122, US)

WHAT PEOPLE SAID AND HOW THEY SAID IT

Yet, despite this emphasis on the visual, when we asked what information from online interactions people used to make the decision to trust, many insisted that the key evidence for deciding whether to trust came from what people said and how they said it: "What were people promising?" "Were they bragging and insincere?" "What did they say they could do; what did they say they couldn't do?" "Was what they were telling me consistent with my research?" "Did they come prepared?" "Did they follow up?" In our initial interviews, managers, especially in the West, told us they paid attention to body language. However, when pressed they admitted that they mostly were using body language as a supplement to interpret what people were saying. In our interviews during COVID-19, without the ability to observe body language, it was what people said and the context in which they said it that interviewees were using to decide to trust.

- *They started by promising something that is too good to be true. And this made me skeptical. I started looking and I discovered that my suspicion was right. What I was going to receive was not as stated in the beginning. This made me, of course, not trust this partner.* (144, Bolivia)
- *It's like if someone's bragging, but there is nothing underneath. If there is true self-confidence, then it's like an energy, but if the self-confidence*

is like narcissistic bragging, then you're just selling something. And that's not sincere. (131, Turkey)

- *I think it's the way people talk. Are people honest? For me it's always a red flag, if someone is only selling the advantages, so isn't really honest about is the disadvantages. Do you have a balanced view, are you honest about the downsides, and not only about the upsides.* (127, Germany)
- *They come informed, prepared; they followed up.* (111, Thailand)

Applying CORR amidst a Pandemic

With constraints on meeting in person and limited visual cues due to meeting online, managers had difficulty acquiring the information they normally used to decide to trust. They described alternative ways of searching for information to judge competence, openness, respect, and rapport, but they were not completely comfortable with the substitutions. It seemed to us that it would be especially difficult to judge respect, the primary standard in the Middle East/South Asia, and rapport, the primary standard in Latin America, online because respect and rapport fundamentally rest on interpretations of intangible information deduced from social interactions and references. Competence, the primary standard in East Asia, and openness, the primary standard in the West, are based on somewhat more tangible information that can be cross-checked. Despite having few alternatives, managers still tried to assess trust standards in the online environment.

Our interviewee from Saudi Arabia told us about a potential investment that he ultimately turned away. One reason was a perceived lack of respect from his potential partners.

We liked the thesis of the investment, we liked the tangible aspects; however, when we met the team, we didn't have the right vibe. We did not like the team and I would say a part of the reason, honestly, they were acting a little bit cocky. We're the investors, but they were like, guys, we can find somebody else. That made us feel that this was definitely not the healthy approach to building a partnership. (136, Saudi Arabia)

Our Latin American interviewees bemoaned the loss of in-person interactions where normally they would judge rapport and decide whether to trust. Recall from chapter 4 that Latin Americans spent considerable time building goodwill before deciding to trust. The pandemic hit Latin American economies hard.[5] The managers we re-interviewed described pivoting. They told us that if their businesses were going to survive, they were going to have to relax their standard of rapport a bit and take risks. The interviewee whom we quoted earlier in this chapter describing how the "beast" of culture nurtured a strong social norm to develop rapport, noted this change in attitude. He went on to say, *Because we have the need of doing business, the Beast of Culture is somehow present but has somehow also lowered. You're not too rigid with this a way of interacting* (144, Bolivia).

As described in chapter 5, East Asians prefer to make a judgment of competence from information gathered during in-person, on-site visits. The relatively short COVID-19 confinement in East Asia meant that managers just postponed the "look-and-see" associated with some opportunities. One interviewee told us about a business opportunity initiated by another company before the COVID-19 limitations were imposed in her country. She did not move forward on the opportunity until she could follow her company's normal process: *Once we did the "look and see" we learned that all their decisions were made by one man. Well, it ended up that we did not work together* (111, Thailand). In another instance, when the East Asian "look-and-see" was not possible, the interviewee told us that his company turned to a broker to vouch for competence: *In order for us to see that potential company is highly competent, we asked the trusted third-party company* (118, Japan).

In the West, managers used online meetings to test for openness. They were looking for reciprocity of information and for follow-up on points made during the online meeting to decide to trust. Two examples:

- (Online) *I think you have to be much more deliberate in in the way you share information. Talking about the negotiations that my team is in now. I'm going to show one of my cards and the expectation is you should show me one of yours. If you do, chances are, I'm likely to show you another one to further the conversation. But if I show you my first card and you choose to just take that information and not reciprocate with some additional information from your side that helps me understand your perspective, well then I'm going to start playing things much more close to the vest. The way you share important information throughout the negotiation becomes much more deliberate and very, very specific.* (122, US)
- *And you have to follow through on everything. That is important in any environment, whether it's pandemic or not. And it is really becoming a lost art. It is not uncommon for me to ask a supplier for three or four pieces of data and then have to ask again and again and again and never get a complete answer. I find myself developing trust faster with someone who just answers all my questions in a timely manner than I do with someone I may have hit it off with if they don't follow up, It takes a little time and effort, but it's so easy to do. And it makes such a big impression, at least on me and I think on a lot of others.* (142, US)

It is too simplistic to say that judging a culturally normative trust standard became more difficult when in-person interaction moved online. The above quotes, as well as our overall impressions from the interviews, imply that moving from in-person to online interaction put new pressures on making the trust decision. Although managers were actively trying to mitigate risk, our sense was that in the Middle East/

South Asia and East Asia, as well as in the West, the conditions imposed by the COVID-19 pandemic meant taking fewer risks. In Latin America, it meant taking greater risks.

Mitigating Risk

Interviewees reported a variety of actions they were taking to mitigate risk and keep their businesses going during the pandemic. One common approach was to expand relationships with current partners. One interviewee, who expressed a lot of frustration about her inability to develop new business during the pandemic, nevertheless described how her company was able to trade on its reputation with a subsidiary of a large potential customer to expand its business.

> *A current German customer introduced us to its Austrian subsidiary. And we had a good season with the Austrians. But then, there was a corporate realignment and I thought we might lose all of this company's business. Instead, new management at the top, who we had not worked with before, reached out to say they want to continue with us next year.* (172, Italy)

Other interviewees described how their companies were generating new business with old customers by helping them adapt to the new online reality.

- *We're building some online tools to help them sell their products. It helps sell our product, but also helps them sell all the products that they carry. That helped us expand our business with them because they see that we're out to help them. That it's more than just a business, is it's more like trying to help each other survive in this new environment.* (119, Nicaragua)

- *Many customers are now interested in telematics* (the branch of information technology that deals with the long-distance transmission of computerized information) *and solving their technical questions and issues remotely. We have some solutions for that. We have actually got contacts from our customers. They know that there is a provision for telematics in our machine and they asking how to how to turn it on and how to get the most out of it.* (162, Finland)

Some interviewees felt comfortable making smaller adjustments.

The pandemic has not affected our appetite and our activity when it comes to dealing with our existing partners. But definitely, we have shied away from new partnerships or we have committed, I would say less amounts than we typically would like to. There was this transaction that we closed last week. It was the first time that we dealt with this partner, but we really liked the opportunity and we liked the markets and our due diligence was just positive across the board. We were willing to deploy bigger funds into this particular investment opportunity. However, because of our inability to meet the team, face to face, and see the company by our own eyes, we decided to stage our investment. We said we would like to invest a certain amount now and we would like to have the option to invest additional amounts in the future once a face-to-face meeting happens. (136, Saudi Arabia)

Others simply put projects on idle, including East Asians when they could not travel to observe the projects they were interested in. Our interviewee from Hong Kong explained, *I think it is very difficult to convince people to sign a billion dollar deal let's say in Cambodia and not to actually have seen the land or seen the project* (174, Hong Kong). Our interviewee from Finland observed, *During COVID-19 there has been a slowdown in business; many projects went on the idle* (162, Finland).

Moving on to Deciding to Trust in a Post-pandemic Future

The pandemic-related barriers to meeting in person interfered with managers' ability to decide to trust and their capacity to develop new business. Except for China, where the pandemic was relatively quickly controlled and managers were free to travel domestically, managers all over the world regretted their inability to meet potential business partners in person to assess trust. As a result, some managers put developing new business relationships on hold; some doubled down, investing more in tried-and-true relationships even when they had identified potentially more lucrative but untried ones; some got creative and took more risk. Despite differences in strategy for business development, everyone learned to use technology to meet online and to make the most of online opportunities to assess the manager on the other side of the audio or video feed. In the next chapter, we share managers' views of the post-pandemic future of deciding to trust in the context of building new business relationships.

CHAPTER 9

The Future of Searching for Trust

Experience with the economic fallout of the COVID-19 pandemic exposed the managers we re-interviewed to just how vulnerable their companies were to the well-being of the global economy. They were anxious to engage in post-pandemic new business development. They told us that their companies had money to invest but at the same time, in making business development decisions, they were paying heightened attention to the relevance of geopolitical and economic factors, in addition of course to the pandemic. If we had re-interviewed them the during the summer of 2020, after the devastating floods in China, Belgium and Germany, and the US, it seems likely they would also be factoring climate change into their decisions. Managers' heightened attention to geopolitical, economic, and pandemic factors revealed that the process of searching for and deciding to trust a potential new business partner depended not only on the stable cultural factors that are the focus of this book but also on environmental uncertainty – a factor that was not so much on their minds before the pandemic.

Money to Invest and New Initiatives to Invest In

Apart from East Asia, new business stagnated during the pandemic. Case in point, China was the only major world economy with a positive 2020 growth rate (2.3 percent). Vietnam and Taiwan also had positive growth rates in 2020; no other countries did.[1] Negative growth rates outside of East Asia reflect what we reported in chapter 8 from managers in Latin America, the West, and Middle East/South Asia. The pandemic had taken a toll on new business. Looking to a post-pandemic future, managers in these regions were optimistic. They were confident that there was money sitting on the sidelines, just waiting to be invested,[2] and they saw new opportunities for investment revealed by the way working and living had changed during the pandemic.

One interviewee well positioned to comment on the global economy had an optimistic view of the post-pandemic future for business development.

In terms of a global business, but there is massive amount of dry powder (he means cash) *just sitting on the on the sideline that I think is waiting to be deployed. When you look at the big players in the market. There are hundreds of billions, and even trillions, that are just sitting as cash in money market funds. And I think all this cash, especially coupling it with all the government incentives, fiscal and otherwise, I think we're going to see a massive boom as soon as life is back to normal. And of course, this is fully reliant on what happens with the vaccines and their actual efficacy on a massive scale.* (136, Saudi Arabia)

Another interviewee, who also thought there was cash waiting to be deployed, pointed out the new ways of working and living necessitated by the pandemic revealed many opportunities for new business. *We say inshallah* (God willing). *Once when all this pandemic finishes, I think we'll see a huge cash flow movement between industries, because people will bring everything they were trying to do during the pandemic to life* (151, Palestine).

Yet another interviewee in the food industry gave a specific example of new peer relationships built during the pandemic that promised more cooperation in a post-pandemic future. At the beginning of the pandemic, the interviewee mentioned, *Everybody was on the same boat* (172, Italy). Consumers, fearful of getting COVID-19 from touching fruits and vegetables an infected person had touched, refrained from purchasing from open bins. Suppliers were all affected similarly, and the interviewee added, *In this case, everybody could help each other* (172, Italy). This same interviewee further explained that working together to overcome consumer resistance strengthened relationships among peer companies and built new relationships for her and her family's business. On the downside, she also noted that gains in sustainable packaging rolled back to 2018 levels.

The Geopolitical Situation

Managers' optimism that the availability of capital and ideas would trigger economic growth was tempered with concern with how various geopolitical situations would impact on developing new business in some parts of the world. At the top of the list were our Hong Kong and Chinese interviewees' concerns about the US–China situation. Would the US continue to impose tariffs on about $360 billion worth of Chinese imports? Would the US impose new, different tariffs or institute a quid-pro-quo whereby the US would lift tariffs in exchange for human rights measures?

- *People in East Asia, especially China, are more cautious on doing business with companies that might have a high potential of being caught in a second or third wave of sanctions by the US. So, there are a lot of projects that have been delayed and this is affecting a lot of business in East Asia right now particularly in Hong Kong and China.* (174, Hong Kong)

- *A big change in addition to what COVID has done may be due to the geopolitical conflict between China and US. I think it is natural people not trusting US companies, because they are afraid that they will get a deal, then it is stopped or interrupted by some political event. Doing a deal with US company, you don't know if those other sanctions will be imposed; whereas, if you do business with a country in Asia, that can be much more reliable.* (189, China)

The managers we interviewed had some good experiences during the pandemic in making alternative arrangements for products and services due to supply chain disruptions, but they also had or knew others who had some bad experiences. The common problem was being able to check out the legitimacy of a company during the pandemic. One manager told of taking extraordinary measures, which included involving his country's ambassador, to check out the legitimacy of a company offering to sell his organization badly needed personal protective equipment. A manager from Palestine took a risk sourcing from a company he could not check out using normal procedures. That did not turn out well and he concluded that it was simply too risky doing new business with companies in some countries. *Some companies start in countries because the rules there are more easy. It's really hard to make sure that this is a real company, not a fraud. Coming from there,* (he's referring to a potential partner) *I would think, three, four times before even agreeing to have a meeting with them* (151, Palestine).

There was also a bright side to recent geopolitical shifts. While discussing the 2020 normalization agreement between the UAE and Israel, one of our interviewees made two important points. First, he explained, *Three months ago a business project between an Israeli and an Emirati was really difficult because there was no mutual way to communicate – there were no direct phone lines.* The normalization agreement brought down structural and cultural barriers: *The second day after the announcement of the agreement between Israel and the United Arab Emirates. I think there were I don't know how many (new) projects between UAE and Israelis* (115, Palestine).

The Post-Pandemic Future

While trying to keep their businesses going despite the pandemic, managers learned that with newly improved video-conferencing technology they could do more online than they first thought – and effectively, too. Although managers recognized that they could use online technology for parts of new business development post COVID-19, they expressed a strong preference for bringing back in-person meetings.

WHAT WORKED ONLINE AND MAY LEAD TO PERMANENT CHANGE

Managers described how having been forced by the pandemic to eliminate travel and work online versus not get the job done generated new efficiencies and identified new capabilities. Our interviews uncovered examples of what may become permanent changes in the way companies do business. Perhaps our biggest supporter of working online was from Palestine. Although recognizing that *people want to go back to normal life,* he thought, *when it comes to the business side, the whole pandemic thing showed people that they can do literally any kind of business they want online. The sky's the limit. You can do whatever you want* (151, Palestine).

Many managers commented on how travel restrictions had changed their ways of doing business. One of many of our frequent traveler interviewees explained the time saved by not traveling. *People are actually finding it* (meeting online) *much more efficient, including myself. I spend so much time traveling. Normally for a two-hour meeting in the US, I spent three days or four days at least. Now you can just do it in two hours and go on with your life. So, I think people realize it's more efficient* (127, Germany). Another manager explained that the pandemic travel restrictions meant that his company, a manufacturer of industrial equipment, was putting more responsibility on its dealers to do installations. Whereas before COVID-19 he would have engineers from headquarters go all over the world to do the installations, during COVID-19, headquarter engineers used video meetings to coach their dealers to do installations. *Now we are relying much more to our dealer network and on the customers. So of course, there's more risk for something going wrong. We need to put more emphasis on double checking the terms and ensuring that all the parties are understanding all the things in same way and we are speaking the same language* (162, Finland). We wondered if the pandemic had changed his company's business model permanently. When we asked if he would still be using the dealers for installations after COVID-19, he acknowledged that was likely at least for some installations. Yet another manager commented on how travel restrictions had changed the Chinese custom of finalizing a new business relationship by having senior managers meet in person and "do the chop" (sign the agreement). This rather formal signing ritual sends an important signal of senior management's commitment to the new business. Rather than forgo the signing ritual due to travel restrictions, our interviewee told us, *for the past few months, they start to accept the way* (online signing) *to completing some deals* (174, Hong Kong).

GENERATIONAL CHALLENGES

Globally, there are many family businesses still run by the generation that built the business with personal relationships. New communication technology can be a challenge for the senior leadership of these companies; so too is the social distance that technology imposes. Fortunately, many family businesses also involve a younger generation for whom the technology is less challenging. Some of our interviewees were members of that younger generation and they told us about leading their families' businesses online during the pandemic. For the future, they saw the value of building relationships with new business partners in the traditional in-person meetings but anticipated that subsequently they would be able to address problems and communicate decisions using online technology.

- *A good part of the businesses in our country are still family businesses. And in family business there are two generations. I think that there will be a very strong need to go back* (to in-person meetings) *from the older generation that is used to have this personal content, this traditional way of doing business. But, now because of the COVID-19 this older person knows that his son is very capable of dealing with the online environment. And that's why I think it's going to be a hybrid, but it will depend on if they have seen the benefit of it* (doing business online). (144, Bolivia)
- *The old generation is still insisting that we could survive without this technology. I'm actually not sure we could survive. I heard it from my father, many, many times. He's complaining, "You're not with us, you're with your phone, but not with us." But to be honest, when it's the time to save a deal or to make a serious business decision then my father first would ask me, "What do you think, can you send email or do something?"* (115, Palestine)
- *I don't think the in-person will ever disappear. My family, my uncle, my dad, they would go in person to everything because they have grown up this way and they know how to talk to the producer. I think in the near future, we'll have a kind of a mixture. Maybe all these two, three generations will try to balance it.* (172, Italy)
- *Here in Europe, our customers, the vast majority, it's family-owned businesses. I see with the next generation coming in people are getting used to this* (working online) *now pretty quickly.* (127, Germany)

THE HYBRID FUTURE OF BUILDING NEW BUSINESS RELATIONSHIPS

The major conclusion from our pre-pandemic interviews was that to decide to trust, managers wanted to meet in person whether in the context of goodwill building or testing. The managers we re-interviewed during the pandemic (fall of 2020) saw the future of deciding to trust a new business partner as some mix of in-person and online meetings. As they were anticipating a future that they had not yet experienced, what aspects of new business development they expected to be in person versus online varied.

One interviewee anticipated making the decision to meet in person versus online on a case-by-case basis. He also made the important point that the pandemic had stretched on so long and people had become so comfortable with online technology that habits would change.

> I think it's going to go back some of the way towards the way it was with in-person meetings, but I don't think it'll ever get there again. The pandemic is going to stretch on far too long. And you're going to develop new habits and new strategies and new communication tools that you're going to get used to and comfortable enough with. And in lots of cases, you're going to find that it's good enough. It's not as important for me to be in person in some of those cases where I would have in the past. It's not as good as being in person, but it provides me an opportunity to better use my time and not have to make every single trip that I made in the past. (142, US)

Another interviewee thought that first steps with potential partners could be done online, likening them to online dating.

> We'll maybe (do more) online after COVID-19, but I don't think it'll be just an online thing, because we're human. Everybody wants to go back to what we used to do but still there are some meetings that both parties

understand, we can have online. Maybe you can take the very first steps
online, what before was on email, now it's online dating. (172, Italy)

Another interviewee thought first and last steps might need to be in
person but the middle ones might be online.

I think we will end up in sort of a hybrid world where it's some of both.
You know businesses are looking for ways to save on expenses and cre-
ate more efficiency. There's been a ton of travel time built into our sched-
ules and those things can come out with more virtual meetings. Nothing
is as good as being in front of someone in person, but you'll save that for
the closing meeting. We'll do two meetings in person instead of four in
person. And we'll do the two in the middle, virtually. (123, US)

In Latin America and the Middle East/South Asia, managers expressed a strong preference to move back to in-person meetings for
new business development. An interviewee from Latin America commented, *After the pandemic people will keep travel and entertainment*
resources only for the fundamental face-to-face meetings with a new part-
ner (183 Uruguay). Our interviewee from Turkey was adamant: *When*
it comes to building new business relations, it's going to go back (to in
person). If you're only sitting in front of a laptop you need interaction, it's
the same for business (131, Turkey).

Our interviewees in East Asia had a much less restricted pandemic experience from that of managers in other regions of the world. Recall, they told
us that whereas international travel was restricted, domestic travel was not;
people were working in their offices and small in-person meetings were possible. In addition, according to one interviewee, *Even before the COVID-19*
there was already wide adoption for such a kind of technology in China. He
went on to say there had been *a sharp increase in adoption of the technology*
(that was already) *most popular in the commercial world, because during the*
COVID all the schools and had to put their courses online (189, China).

One interviewee from Singapore acknowledged the value of video conferencing but also the need people had to meet in person. *I think the video conferences help to facilitate more ongoing conversations and all that it is helpful, but I think there is still a really high preference for face-to-face meetings, especially in Asia Pacific in Japan.* (143, Singapore). To emphasize her conclusion about how important it is to people to meet in person, she told us about an online meeting in which the presenters decided to be in the same room.

We were holding a user group a meeting and everyone was on video. We were having our customer and one of our partners and an employee talk in a panel. Even though everybody (the user group) *was virtual, they* (presenters) *still wanted to do the panel conversation face to face, because they thought that there's a lot more chemistry when you actually do it face to face. It was a very funny, so you've got everybody* (the three presenters) *sitting like 1.5 meters apart with screens* (between them). *They've got their masks on. Like total social distancing, but they were in the same room actually having a conversation.* (143, Singapore)

Culture Will Outlast the Pandemic

The pandemic taught us just how globally interconnected our societies and our economies are. We got COVID-19 from each other and gave COVID-19 to each other. Economic contagion spreads just as quickly as the virus – no single economy escaped unharmed. Technology made it possible to keep business going; it even made it possible to develop new business in some instances. Nevertheless, our conclusion from the fall 2020 interviews was that in response to the pandemic, technology did not wipe out cultural differences. Trust was part of the cultural story but so was tightness-looseness. Regional cultural differences in trust and tightness-looseness generated mostly predictable and occasionally surprising regional differences in how people went about the decision to trust during the pandemic.

TIGHT, HIGH-TRUST, EAST ASIAN CULTURES

As we described at the beginning of this chapter, tight, high-trust East Asian cultures weathered the pandemic better than other cultural regions with respect to health and economic outcomes. To be sure, East Asians were more prepared for COVID-19 than other regions of the world because of their experience with SARS almost two decades earlier. Their governments, taking advantage of the widespread use of technology, initiated a swift and all-encompassing societal response. People complied (a tight culture effect). Business, even new business development, although limited by restrictions on international travel, restarted.

In the fall of 2020, our East Asian interviewees emphasized that the old practices for deciding to trust, such as seeking information about potential partners' reputations and brokers' recommendations, continued to be core practices.

- *Introductions are core; very bread and butter.* (143, Singapore)
- *A lot of commercial customs (in China) are running pretty well the same as in Europe or United States, but of course that private relationship still makes sense. Especially when you start new things and then you need to call your friends or insiders to learn, who in this industry has the best-in-class reputation. Still, that is the main thing you would do.* (189, China)
- *Competencies. Actually, that is our first priority, of course, but it is quite difficult for us to evaluate degree of competency before (meeting with them). Now, we generally ask the trusted third-party company.* (118, Japan)

Mangers in this region preferred to test competence, their primary CORR standard for deciding to trust in person, on site. In some cases, they could continue to do so. In other cases when they could not travel, they had a fall back to brokering. If their broker was on site and could assure competence, people in this region had a basis for taking the risk to trust a new partner.

LOOSE, HIGH-TRUST, WESTERN CULTURES

The West, with its loose but high-trust culture, managed COVID-19 poorly. Loose culture is a major driving factor in the lack of compliance with public health measures in many Western cultures.[3] Despite this, three factors appear to have contributed to maintaining business development in this region: high trust, a quick pivot to online interaction, and the realization that the openness sought before COVID-19 via in-person testing could be judged online by assessing willingness to share information, transparency of pros and cons, and reciprocity.

In the initial round of interviews, reported in chapter 6, Westerners often said they judged their key CORR standard, openness, by reading body language, observing eye contact, assessing strength of handshakes, and so on. However, when we inquired about what they were looking for in the body language, what inferences they were drawing, they told us testing for openness came down to whether a potential partner was transparent and willing to reciprocate information, and whether the information supplied by the potential partner converged with other available information about the partner. Although testing moved online with the pandemic, the perceived importance of this standard did not change. Moreover, people realized that they did not have to be in person to gather the information they needed to judge openness successfully.

- *I think the key to building trust is no different in a COVID world versus a non-COVID world. And I think that is transparency, being upfront admitting what you're working on. People are much more understanding of an area that is not perfect for you as an organization. If you admit, hey, here's a place where we're not perfect and here's what we're doing to improve it, then if you don't speak of it and try to act as if it's not there. So being transparent, being upfront about who you are, where your strengths are and then what you can do and being willing to listen and get that same sort of transparent truth from any potential business partner. Those are things that will really make a difference.* (123, US)

- *During COVID-19, building trust still matters. It just moved online. Probably all of us thought you have to meet a person and you have to have dinner together in order to build a relationship. But we realized trust happens over what we do. It's the way people talk. Are people honest? For me it's always a red flag, if someone only sees the advantages and isn't really honest about the disadvantages.* (127, Germany)

Ultimately, Western, high-trust cultures were using the same indicators when making the trust decision online as they had been using in person. What was different during the pandemic, as discussed thoroughly in chapter 8, was the difficulty managers in Western cultures had in making contacts for new business. Pre-pandemic, loose culture facilitated making contacts in informal "meet-ups." Without those opportunities, managers in Western cultures told us they were relying more on networks for introductions.

LOOSE, LOW-TRUST, LATIN AMERICAN CULTURES

Loose, low-trust, Latin American cultures struggled to manage the harsh health effects of COVID-19 and the resulting severe economic downturn. The primary trust standard in this region, rapport, is very difficult to judge exclusively from online interaction. It was our impression from the interviews that, at the outset of the pandemic, businesses in this region were not as advanced in using online technology as those in other regions, in particular East Asia. Latin American interviewees observed that it was not just a question of pivoting to using technology, but that their cultures had to change fundamentally in the face of the pandemic-induced economic downturn. One interviewee explained, *right now, what I perceive is a lot of uncertainty. And that uncertainty makes the values change* (144, Bolivia).

People in loose cultures innovate in the face of uncertainty.[4] The change associated with deciding to trust a potential business partner was loosening adherence to traditional business practices of vetting trust in prolonged in-person, goodwill building social encounters to judge rapport. Although changes in the process of deciding to trust were made from necessity, not preference, our Latin American interviewees tended to see the changes as positive and likely to be permanent. Recall our interviewee from Bolivia who talked about the Beast of Culture: *The barriers have gone down in terms of how much I need to know you personally. So it's like the beast ... is somehow present but has also lowered* (144, Bolivia).

TIGHT, HETEROGENEOUS, MIDDLE EASTERN AND SOUTH ASIAN CULTURES

Heterogeneity and tightness plus low trust made generating new business during the pandemic in the Middle East and South Asia extremely difficult. Generating new inter-regional business was already challenging before COVID-19 because it required overcoming prejudices and risk. One interviewee who had done pre-pandemic business with Israeli companies explained, *Doing business with an Israeli is kind of like betraying your own group by doing business with the enemy of the people* (115, Palestine). Deciding to trust in this region came only after in-person goodwill building in which gestures of hospitality graciously offered and humbly received provided sufficient evidence of respect of differences. This type of social interaction simply could not be done during the pandemic. Low trust, and relatively little experience with online meetings prior to the pandemic, made it difficult for many people in this region to pivot to building trust without that crucial in-person interaction. There was a strong desire to return to in-person meetings, *You know, in terms of adopting to doing everything over the video, I think they do it to the extent where it's a necessity, rather than a choice to change* (101, Kuwait).

Our sense was that in the low-trust, tight Middle Eastern cultures, the common response to the disruption of normal business due to the pandemic was to minimize risk by holding off on initiating new projects. In contrast, in the low-trust, loose Latin American cultures, the common response was to relax CORR trust standards and take more risk. Many factors, of course, contribute to these differences, and we only talked to a small number of observers in each region, but one cultural difference that stands out as a partial explanation is tightness-looseness. The looser Latin American cultures met the crisis by loosening standards to engage in new business activity, whereas the tighter Middle Eastern cultures chose instead to maintain their standards by limiting new business activity until it could proceed under the guidance of normal standards.

Moving on to Applying Insights

Although the pandemic of 2020 was a major global shock, it did not fundamentally change culture and it did not fundamentally change the CORR standards that managers use to decide to trust a new business partner. It did affect managers' ability to meet in person to assess competence, openness, respect, and rapport. Some changes made in response to the pandemic will endure but, just as there seems to be money to invest, there seems to be pent-up desire to meet in person to develop new business relationships. Thus, the practical advice in the final chapter of this book draws heavily on the CORR standards and key actions for deciding to trust that we developed from the original interviews and on our cultural explanation for regional differences in reliance on standards and actions based on trust and tightness-looseness.

CHAPTER 10

Points of Application – How to Maximize Insights from This Book

The central theme of this book is the importance of trust for developing new business relationships around the world and how two cultural factors – trust and tightness-looseness – affect the way people in different cultures decide to trust. In this chapter, we share our perspective on how to apply the insights from this book. We offer practical tools and tips for performing the key actions for searching for information to decide to trust: due diligence, brokering, testing, and goodwill building. We advise you on how to meet potential partners' standards of trust: competence, openness, respect, rapport – CORR. We discuss how to use cultural knowledge to identify when actions that on the surface might seem disrespectful are cultural and how to respond. Finally, we provide some caveats regarding the generalizability of our evidence-based insights based on deciding to trust a business partner to deciding to trust in other contexts.

Searching for Trust: Key Actions for Gathering Information

We identified four key actions managers use searching for information to decide to trust: due diligence, brokering, testing, and goodwill building. Because searching for information is a critical part of the process of deciding to trust, we offer practical advice for each.

DUE DILIGENCE

With the click of a button, an individual can access the internet and learn a great deal about you, including your work history (e.g., current and/or previous employer) and information not related to work (e.g., relationship status, siblings). In the process of deciding to trust, managers, and people in general, often turn to the internet for information about others. Therefore, it is important to be aware of what information is on your professional pages (e.g., LinkedIn), and on social media. When it comes to information you can control, try to ensure that it puts you in a good light. For example, if most of your language on social media is self-focused (i.e., I, me, mine) and most of your pictures place you at the center of attention, someone might perceive that you may be inclined to act in self-serving ways in the context of a partnership. Using another example, if some of your posts and comments on social media are about how others have incorrect worldviews, someone might perceive that you may be intolerant of views that are different from your own.

Recognize that not all the information about you and/or your organization available online is likely to be positive. If you get the chance, be prepared to address a not-so-positive past. Blaming others is not likely to be effective in allaying a potential partner's concerns. Instead, be open and transparent in responding to questions about negative reputational information, provide an explanation where necessary, and focus on what you can contribute to the potential relationship and what you see the other party contributing.

At the end of the day, managers all over the world prefer to rely on their own interpersonal experience to make the decision to trust. Even during the pandemic, when in-person interaction was extremely limited, managers were reluctant to trust others whom they had not met in person. If there is negative information about you or your company, if feasible, try to get a meeting in person and address it.

BROKERING

As we learned in previous chapters, in certain cultural regions, such as East Asia and Middle East/South Asia, an introduction from a third party who can connect you to a potential partner is a good first step in building trust with a potential partner. However, it is important to keep two things in mind when it comes to third-party brokers. First, be sure that the third party you are approaching to make the introduction is someone whom you and your potential partner trust. A brokered introduction carries significantly more weight when the person making the introduction is a trusted contact. Second, recognize that in some cultures, for example in East Asia, it may be difficult for a broker to be direct and explicit about the dangers of working with a potential partner. Thus, pay attention to contextual information that the third party is providing about the potential partner. For example, in an East Asian culture, a broker saying modest things about a potential partner may be the broker's way of signaling that the potential partner may not be a good fit for you. Chances are that the broker is being indirect and issuing you a forewarning not to work with a potential partner!

TESTING

In cultural regions such as the West and East Asia, testing is a normal part of the process of deciding to trust a potential partner. In such cultures, expect to be tested most likely via a lot of questions that may seem to cover the same ground. Trying to sidestep questions may be a good skill for politicians but is not wise when you want to build a business, or any other kind of relationship based on trust. It is important not to take testing personally or as a signal of distrust. People who use testing extensively are usually from high-trust regions. They assume others are trustworthy, but they want to be sure, so they test. Managers engaged in testing are not trying to catch you lying; they are trying to confirm their assumption that you are trustworthy.

Recognize what you are being tested for – it's going to be different in the West and in East Asia – and demonstrate it. For example, in the West you are most likely being tested for openness, whereas in East Asia, you are most likely being tested for competency.

At the same time, in cultural regions where managers engage in testing it is perfectly appropriate for you to test in return. Testing can be a two-way street. However, how you test in direct-communication, Western culture, and indirect-communication, East Asian culture, probably should be different. Where you can be direct in Western culture, you may need to be more circumspect in East Asian culture.

GOODWILL BUILDING

Social interactions focused on getting to know a potential partner are a prerequisite for deciding to trust in cultural regions such as the Middle East/South Asia and Latin America. If you are considering working with someone from these regions, expect to be invited to social events in which you are shown hospitality. Recognize that while these are social events, you also are being assessed. Accept hospitality graciously and be curious and ask questions to learn more about neutral topics, for example, local food or local sporting events. Ask for advice about what you should see, visit, eat, while in their city and country. You are likely to receive an invitation to be shown around. You can gradually move to discussing business but, if you are from the West, the social conversation may extend much longer than you are used to in your own culture. Be patient; do not try to push the conversation to the potential business relationship prematurely. Recognize that in some cultures, if the personal relationship is not there, people will not be very interested in a business relationship.

Know that your personal values and your business values are important to the potential partner who will be trying to learn about you during these social interactions. If possible, show hospitality in return, perhaps by inviting your host and potential partner to visit you in return.

Sharing a meal is one of the most common ways to offer and accept hospitality. Although it may seem like a small matter to choose to eat alone especially if fatigued by travel, declining an invitation to eat with a potential partner can highlight a sense of separateness and may send negative signals about the potential for collaboration and a high-quality relationship. When you share a meal, be prepared to at least taste some unusual foods. Different customs about alcohol can be a challenge. Be prepared to follow the lead of your host, but if you do not drink alcohol, just explain why you don't. Most reasons – religious, health – will be respected.

Deciding to Trust: CORR Standards

When these four key actions – due diligence, brokering, testing, and goodwill building – are performed appropriately, they can uncover important information about the CORR standards – competence, openness, respect, and rapport – that managers use in deciding to trust a potential business partner. Given the importance of each standard for deciding to trust, we offer practical advice for each.

COMPETENCE

In East Asia, a failure to demonstrate competence can be a major obstacle when deciding to trust. Therefore, come to meetings prepared – bring data, hard facts, proof of accomplishments, and credentials – and expect the same of your potential partner. When both parties provide evidence that they can deliver, each can have more confidence that they can have a high-quality business relationship.

We should note that competence also involves bringing the right person of the right status to the meeting. Doing so signals the organization's commitment to the project. East Asian interviewees first raised the issue of people feeling slighted when the potential partner did not follow this norm. However, during the pandemic, with meetings online, interviewees in the West saw the value of signaling commitment to a project by bringing in high-level managers, which of course was much easier because of remote conferencing technology. You can use due diligence to uncover information about the rank of the people potentially participating in a meeting. The goal is to have people of close to equal rank attending. If you plan to bring your manager or your manager's manager to a meeting, it is best to let the partner know well in advance. Don't fail to thoroughly brief your managers on what you need them to say and do in those meetings. The objective for you and for your potential partner is no surprises that might lead to embarrassment. Embarrassment happens if your potential partner doesn't have managers of the same rank at the meeting and when the managers you bring are not thoroughly briefed on the role they are supposed to play. Matching ranks, especially in hierarchical cultures, such as East Asia and the Middle East/South Asia where deference to higher-status people is stronger than in the West or Latin America,[1] signals both sides' commitment to the joint project.

OPENNESS

Sharing information as openly and honestly as possible can make or break relationships in Western cultures. Expect to be asked questions about past performance and about your vision for the future business relationship. Be prepared to share and, when you cannot share, to explain why not or at what stage of the process of deciding to trust you could share information, which in the meantime must remain confidential. Your partner may interpret your reluctance to share information as a signal that you are hiding something. When you openly share information, when you explain why you cannot share, or when you explain the circumstances under which you could share, you are demonstrating your trustworthiness by recognizing trust is a two-way street. At the same time, it's all right, actually expected, that you ask the other party questions about their vision of the potential business relationship. By asking, you are signaling your engagement. By answering, your potential partner is demonstrating trustworthiness. As parties continue to exchange information about their potential business relationship, they should begin to see whether the project they had in mind is viable. Even if the conclusion is that this is not a project for us at this time, the open information sharing may have established the basis for a future project.

RESPECT

When meeting with potential partners in the Middle East/South Asia, show respect by offering and accepting hospitality. Recall that this region has many different subcultures associated with tribe, religion, and so forth. Managers in this region are sensitive to social differences, so it is important to show you respect those differences. A good way to do so is to graciously offer and accept hospitality. You are honoring the potential partner and, in this region, honor – a person' reputation – is the basis for self-worth.[2] Thus, by showing hospitality you are honoring them and signaling, "I respect who you are, even if we are different." Respect goes a long way in establishing a foundation for a high-quality relationship characterized by trust.

It is all right to set limits. In fact, that is part of the process of assessing respect.[3] The key is to demonstrate that you respect the potential partner as a person worthy of honor even if the potential partner follows practices that are different from yours. There are many examples of respecting differences in our section on hospitality in chapter 3. The examples make the point that showing respect does not mean you have to imitate or copy, but that showing respect does mean you should acknowledge and accept the difference. Of course, if you discover the potential partner has values that you consider unethical, you may wish to end the meeting politely and perhaps a little sooner than if their values were ones you could respect.

RAPPORT

When meeting with potential partners from Latin America, be prepared to spend considerable social time together having coffee, tea, or meals; attending sporting events; taking in the local sites. When together be sure to ask questions that facilitate building an interpersonal relationship. Social psychologists have specific exercises and questions that help people quickly learn information about others and develop interpersonal closeness.[4] After getting to know each other, for example by sharing information about family and background, you might feel comfortable enough to ask questions to generate interpersonal closeness, such as those in exhibit 10.1.

EXHIBIT 10.1. *Questions to generate interpersonal closeness and start a conversation leading to a business relationship.*
What does friendship mean to you?
What do you value most in a friendship?
What do you value most in a business partnership?
What does a business relationship mean to you?

The answers to such questions about personal and business values could uncover important information about whether you share values sufficiently to develop rapport with a potential partner, or they might just lead directly to rapport.

The Benefits of Cultural Knowledge

Conflict in intercultural relationships often is due to differences in cultural norms and standards. You may feel offended when someone from a different culture violates your cultural norms. However, consider the possibilities for trusting relationships if such violations can be avoided, or at least understood as behavior that, although not normative in your culture, is perfectly acceptable in the other party's culture. This is one of the major benefits of cultural knowledge. Stated differently, if you know what is culturally appropriate and normative in another culture, you can anticipate and correctly interpret the behavior of a person from that culture. Of course, having cultural knowledge does not mean you can "jump the line" or circumvent the trust process, but cultural knowledge should allow you to effectively navigate the process of searching for and deciding to trust.

What is the best way to generate cultural knowledge? Guides[5] provide a lot of good advice, and you will benefit from having done some cultural as well as reputational due diligence. However, guides are not always available and don't always cover the situation in which you find yourself. To increase your preparation to make the decision to trust regardless of your own and your potential partner's culture, we recommend building cultural intelligence.

Cultural intelligence (CQ) is the ability to understand, act, and manage effectively in culturally diverse settings.[6] People whose CQ is high have general knowledge about cultural differences, such as available in this book, but they take it a step further, recognizing differences as cultural, having the motivation to find solutions to cultural challenges, and having the ability to adjust their own behavior to cultural conditions.[7] Although this sounds daunting, actually it is not. CQ, like any ability, will improve with practice and active engagement in education about culture, travel, international assignments, as well as intercultural experiences.[8]

When we talk to managers and students about the value of cultural knowledge, someone inevitably asks, "Why me? Why do I have to do all the cultural work?" Our answer is you don't, but you may have to initiate the process because it is easier for people from loose cultures than from tight cultures to engage in cultural adjustment. Review the sections on cultural tightness-looseness in chapter 2. Recall that in loose cultures, norms are less strict than in tight cultures. People have to figure out what norm is operating in the context. People in loose cultures have to engage in behavioral flexibility and improvisation more than people in tight cultures. Are you from a tight or loose culture? Take Gelfand's Tight-Loose Mindset Quiz to learn more about yourself.[9]

The cultural differences we have identified in the process of searching for and deciding to trust in new business relationships set traps into which managers and others may fall into unless they apply their CQ. Exhibit 10.2 identifies some of these traps and gives some advice for avoiding them or extracting yourself once trapped.

EXHIBIT 10.2. *Traps in the process of searching for and deciding to trust.*

- If you are suspicious of East Asians' indirectness, avoid saying, "Just tell me if you can do this project or not!" Instead, suggest there are challenges in completing any project and ask what the other person sees as the challenges. If they cannot talk about challenges, maybe they are not the right partner for you.
- If you feel reluctant to reciprocate Westerners' openness, reframe your thinking away from the thought, "They will use what I share to take advantage of me." Provide a little non-damaging information. Ask for some information in return. Reciprocity builds trust.
- If you feel bored with East Asians' demonstrations of com-petence (e.g., facts, historical data), resist the temptation to

interject, "I know you are competent; that's why I'm talking to you!" Remember in a culture where it is difficult to say no directly, sharing information about competence is an indirect way of showing you what they can do and what they cannot or have not done.

- If you feel impatient with prolonged goodwill building in Latin America (e.g., extensive lunch conversations about family), the Middle East/South Asia (e.g., three cups of tea and conversation about non-business-related items), refrain from uttering, "Let's just get to business!" Remember why they are doing this. Refocus yourself on building a personal relationship and enjoy learning about them and their culture.

- If you feel reticent about discussing personal values or life choices in Latin America, understand the consequence of saying, "That's personal, not business!" is that they lose trust in you. In these cultures, the personal relationship is the basis for trust. When there is no personal relationship underlying the business relationship in Latin America, don't count on trust to smooth over the inevitable challenges that confront new relationships.

- If you fail to respect hierarchy, especially in East Asia and the Middle East/South Asia, expect others to become frustrated, as they might think but not directly say, "I want to talk to someone who has authority, not a figurehead!" Be prepared to involve people on your side whose status in your organization is equal to the status of those representing the potential partner. Keep in mind that your organization may be large and theirs may be small, but if they are involving their president or managing director, use technology to engage someone of equal status on your side.

- If you feel offended by Westerners' directness, casualness, and equitable ways, recognize that they are trying to be honest and open with you in the hope that you will do the same. Share a little non-damaging information. Ask them to share in turn. Go slow, get comfortable with their process.

- Avoid interpreting an East Asian broker's subdued introduction as a direct sign of approval. What East Asian brokers don't say is as important as what they do say. Read the context; evaluate the level of enthusiasm displayed.
- If asked to do something that you think is ethically questionable, recognize that you can and should set limits.
- If you are in a situation where norms strongly encourage you to show respect for local standards, try not to default to, "I'm not going to do that!" unless of course doing so would violate the ethical standards under which you are operating, which include the controlling law, organizational policy, and your own personal standards.

Cultural knowledge can help you avoid these traps. Recognizing and understanding what behavior is cultural cues tolerance for such behavior, provides additional perspective, and can motivate search for a different approach to deciding to trust.

Final Caveats

In closing, we offer a couple final caveats. First, we organized cultures into four regions classified by the World Bank as areas of significant global economic activity. Although these regions and their cultural differences in trust and tightness-looseness offer a simple, easily understandable framework for interpreting the process of searching for and deciding to trust, focusing on such large geographical areas – each containing many different countries and cultures – clearly risks overgeneralizing. Because there is always variability within cultures, you should expect variability within regions with respect to cultural levels of trust and tightness-looseness, as well as preferences for key actions and CORR standards. However, the trust and tightness-looseness that are shared within and between regions provide an abiding and slow-to-change cultural explanation for why managers in different cultural regions go about searching for and deciding to trust differently.

Second, we conducted interviews with managers who were engaged in developing new business relationships – a context where trust is critical due to high levels of uncertainty and vulnerability on the part of each partner. In such a context, there are significant costs when trust is misplaced. Although not every interpersonal relationship involves such high financial stakes, personal relationships do risk emotions, reputations, and, not infrequently, money. Because the decision to trust in a personal relationship occurs in the same cultural context of trust and tightness-looseness as the decision to trust in a new business relationship, we believe that the CORR standards we identified as crucial to the decision to trust in business relationships are also relevant to interpersonal relationships. For example, rapport is an important basis for friendships in Latin America and, just as in business relationships, it is developed during goodwill-building activities. Openness is a key criterion for friendships in the West, just as it is for business. The difference between building a business and an interpersonal relationship is what people are open about – their vision of the business versus their vision of themselves. In East Asia, a person's reputation tells you as much about that person as a friend as about that person as a business associate. In the Middle East/South Asia, making friends across subcultural boundaries requires respect for differences. In short, there are likely to be many cultural similarities in how managers decide to trust potential business partners and how people in everyday social interaction decide to trust.

It is our hope that this book becomes a resource that you refer to time and time again. In fact, we believe that skillful application of the insights from this book can open up possibilities for relationships beyond your world of imagination. Trust us!

Acknowledgments

It is a tall order to write a book on how people in different regions of the world decide to trust others. A project of this magnitude would not be possible without family, friends, and colleagues who have had a profound impact on our personal lives and supported our taking on this research project and then our writing a book about it. We are indebted to the 82 interviewees who contributed their valuable time to share the insights that made the original work possible and the 21 who consented to be re-interviewed about how COVID-19 had affected searching for trust. Each interviewee has a name and a personal story. The interviews gave us a unique opportunity to connect personally, albeit briefly, with each of them. We are grateful to them for sharing their experiences, telling their stories, and answering our interminable *what, why, how* questions. Their insights and especially their stories helped us understand their experiences and organize them into a coherent framework that explains their similarities and differences.

We certainly could not have developed our framework of trust by tightness-looseness to explain regional cultural differences in the process of deciding to trust without the pioneering work and insights about tightness-looseness of Michele Gelfand and the original trust by tightness-looseness framework Jeanne developed with Brian Gunia and Brosh Teucher to explain differences in use of negotiation strategy. Michele, Brian, Brosh, thank you for sharing your scholarship and friendship. We would like to thank Donald Ferrin, Maddy Janssens, Jing Jing Yao, and Helen Schwartzman for meaningful feedback and suggestions on various drafts of our work in progress. We would also like to thank Richard Posthuma, who edited our work for an article in the *International Journal of Conflict Management* and Amy Gallo who edited our work for a *Harvard Business Review* article. We appreciate Adam Rosen's comprehensive developmental editing. We are grateful to our colleagues, whose endorsements support the ideas in this book. Writing a book takes a toll on not only the authors but their families. We so appreciate our family members listening to us when we got frustrated, supporting us when we had deadlines, and believing that our project was worthwhile.

Jeanne M. Brett
Tyree D. Mitchell

Notes

Introduction

1 Numbers in parenthesis refer to the interviewee who was the source of the quote and correspond to exhibit I.1.

2 Our definition is consistent with one of the most widely accepted definitions of trust as an intention to accept vulnerability based on the expectations that one or more individuals will enact a specific behavior. See Mayer, R.C., Davis, J.H., & Schoorman, F.D. (1995). An integrative model of organizational trust. *Academy of Management Review, 20,* 709–34.

3 Deutsch, M. (1973). *The resolution of conflict.* New Haven, CT: Yale University Press.

4 When people trust each other, they use fewer resources to guard themselves from being exploited and they achieve better economic outcomes. Kong, D.T., Dirks, K.T., & Ferrin, D.L. (2014). Interpersonal trust within negotiations: Meta-analytic evidence, critical contingencies, and directions for future research. *Academy of Management Journal, 57,* 1235–55.

5 For a review of research on the universal and culturally specific aspects of trust (e.g., meaning of trust), see Ferrin, D.L., & Gillespie, N. (2010). Trust differences across national-societal cultures: Much to do, or much ado about nothing? In M. Saunders, D. Skinner, G. Dietz, N. Gillespie, & R. Lewicki (Eds.), *Trust across cultures: Theory and practice* (pp. 42–86). Cambridge, UK: Cambridge University Press.

6 The most recent version of the World Values Survey can be accessed by visiting the link included in the reference that follows. Haerpfer, C., Inglehart, R., Moreno, A., Welzel, C., Kizilova, K, Diez-Medrano, J., et al., (2020). World values survey: Round seven-country – pooled datafile. Available at www.worldvaluessurvey.org/WVSDocumentationWV7.jsp

7 The *World Bank Annual Report 2016* can be retrieved from http://documents.worldbank .org/curated/en/782691475489708512/World-Bank-annual-report-2016-organizational -information-and-lending-dataappendixes

8 See Gelfand, M. (2018). *Rule makers, rule breakers: Tight and loose cultures and the secret signals that direct our lives.* New York, NY: Scribner.

9 Our research was published in the *International Journal of Conflict Management* in 2019. Brett, J.M., & Mitchell, T.D. (2019). Searching for trustworthiness: Culture, trust, and negotiating new business relationships. *International Journal of Conflict Management, 31,* 17–39.

10 You can access our *Harvard Business Review* article by visiting the link included in the following reference. Brett, J.M., & Mitchell, T.D. (2020, January 31). Research: How to build trust with business partners from other cultures. *Harvard Business Review.* Retrieved from https://hbr.org/2020/01/research-how-to-build-trust-with-business -partners-from-other-cultures

11 *World Bank Annual Report 2016.*

12 www.kellogg.northwestern.edu/trust-project/videos/by-discipline.aspx
This website is the location of a set of recent videos about trust featuring scholars from disciplines as diverse as bioethics and pediatrics to economics, psychology, and philosophy talking about their research on trust.

13 Ferrin & Gillespie, 2010.

14 Haerpfer et al., 2020.

15 Ferrin & Gillespie, 2010.

16 Lytle, A.L., Brett, J.M., Barsness, Z.I., Tinsley, C.H., & Janssens, M. (1995). A paradigm for confirmatory cross-cultural research in organizational behavior. *Research in organizational behavior: An annual series of analytical essays and critical reviews* (Vol. 17), 167–214.

17 Haerpfer et al., 2020.

18 Using extensive evidence, Michele Gelfand has provided a compelling case for the notion that some cultures adhere more strictly to social norms. Gelfand, M.J., Raver, J.L., Nishii, L., Leslie, L.M., Lun, J., Lim, B.C., ... Yamaguchi, S. (2011). Differences between tight and loose cultures: A 33-nation study. *Science, 332*(6033), 1100–4; Gelfand, M.J., Jackson, J.C., Pan, X., Nau, D., Pieper, D., Denison, E., ... Wang, M. (2021). The relationship between cultural tightness–looseness and COVID-19 cases and deaths: A global analysis. *The Lancet Planetary Health, 5*(3), e135–e144.

19 English was a second language for most of the managers we interviewed. To give you, the reader, a sense of the way they described searching for trust, we kept the quotes from our interviewees in their own voices, refraining from correcting grammar and restricting our editors from doing so.

1. Searching for and Deciding to Trust

1 Qualitative methods are particularly useful when researchers seek to understand the full range of behaviors and attitudes that a context might affect. Our research goal was to gain a more complete understanding of how managers decide to trust a potential new business partner within their own culture. Johns, G. (2006). The essential impact of context on organizational behavior. *Academy of Management Review, 31,* 386–408.

2 The *World Bank Annual Report 2016* can be retrieved from https://documents.worldbank .org/curated/en/782691475489708512/World-Bank-annual-report-2016-organizational -information-and-lending-dataappendixes

3 In analyzing our data, we relied on guidelines offered by Eisenhardt and Graebner (2007) as well as Miles and Huberman (1994) to identify culturally normative actions managers engaged in when searching for information to use in deciding to trust a potential business partner. Eisenhardt, K.M., & Graebner, M.E. (2007). Theory building from cases:

Opportunities and challenges. *Academy of Management Journal, 50,* 25–32; Miles, M.B., & Huberman, A.M. (1994). *Qualitative data analysis.* Beverly Hills, CA: Sage.

4   Nir Halevy, an expert on the topic of brokering, defines brokering as a multifaceted social influence process that can take the form of intermediation (connecting disconnected others) or modification (changing others' preexisting relationships). He points out that a broker's power to change others' relationships is based on the broker's access to information or ability to influence. He also recognizes that a broker can have a positive or a negative influence on others' relationships. Halevy, N., Halali, E., & Zlatev, J.J. (2019). Brokerage and brokering: An integrative review and organizing framework for third-party influence. *Academy of Management Annals, 13,* 215–39.

5   The four key actions we identified are by no means exhaustive of all the different ways people search for information to use to decide to trust. However, they were the key actions that dominated our interviewees' responses to our questions about what people do when searching for information to use in deciding to trust.

6   This is not an exhaustive set of standards for deciding to trust; however, it reflects the standards that our interviewees emphasized.

7   See Ferrin, D.L., & Gillespie, N. (2010). Trust differences across national-societal cultures: Much to do, or much ado about nothing? In M. Saunders, D. Skinner, G. Dietz, N. Gillespie, & R. Lewicki (Eds.), *Trust across cultures: Theory and practice* (pp. 42–86). Cambridge, UK: Cambridge University Press. These authors review the research on the determinants of trust and trustworthy people, concluding that the three characteristics of trustworthiness that are widely used in research are applicable across cultures. These are ability (having the skills to perform successfully), benevolence (intentions to benefit others), and integrity (possessing ethics and principles). Ferrin and Gillespie caution that (1) these three characteristics of trust are not an exhaustive list of characteristics that people use to determine trust; (2) there are culturally and contextually specific manifestations and interpretations of ability, benevolence, and integrity; (3) the three characteristics are not equally important in different trust situations; and (4) the three characteristics are not equally important in different cultures. See also Mayer, R.C., Davis, J.H., & Schoorman, F.D. (1995). An integrative model of organizational trust. *Academy of Management Review, 20,* 709–34.

8   See this recent collection of videos about trust research made by scholars from many disciplines: https://www.kellogg.northwestern.edu/trust-project/videos/by-discipline.aspx See also Doney, P.M., Cannon, J.P., & Mullen, M.R. (1998). Understanding the influence of national culture on the development of trust. *Academy of Management Review, 23,* 601–20; Ferrin & Gillespie, 2010.

9   For insight regarding the relationship between trust and context, see van der Werff, L., & Buckley, F. (2017). Getting to know you: A longitudinal examination of trust cues and trust development during socialization. *Journal of Management, 43,* 742–70. For insight regarding the relationship between trust and culture, see Ferrin & Gillespie, 2010. See also Doney et al., 1998.

10   *World Bank Annual Report 2016.*

11   Gelfand, M. (2018). *Rule makers, rule breakers: Tight and loose cultures and the secret signals that direct our lives.* New York, NY: Scribner.

2. Trust and Tightness-Looseness

1   Fons Trompenaars offered this definition of culture as a functional solution. Trompenaars, F. (1996). Resolving international conflict: Culture and business strategy. *Business Strategy Review, 7,* 51–68.

2 For other examples of how people from various cultures greet each other differently, see Morrison, T., & Conaway, W.A. (2006). *Kiss, bow, or shake hands: The bestselling guide to doing business in more than 60 countries*. Adams Media.

3 Michele Gelfand concludes that because social norms facilitate cooperation, social norms have enabled people to survive extreme environmental conditions (e.g., famine, natural disasters). Gelfand, M. (2018). *Rule makers, rule breakers: Tight and loose cultures and the secret signals that direct our lives*. New York, NY: Scribner.

4 For more information on the differences between tight and loose cultures, see Gelfand, M.J., Nishii, L.H., & Raver, J.L. (2006). On the nature and importance of cultural tightness-looseness. *Journal of Applied Psychology, 91*, 1225–44.

5 A bell curve is a visual representation of a normal probability distribution. Variation around the mean creates the bell shape. Variation represents the distribution of values around a central tendency or mean.

6 Trust is higher in Japan than Brazil. For two resources supporting this, see the online map at the following reference: Ortiz-Ospina, E., & Max Roser, M. (2016). Trust. Retrieved from: https://ourworldindata.org/trust
   See also Inglehart, R., Haerpfer, C., Moreno, A., Welzel, C., Kizilova, K., Diez-Medrano, J., Lagos, M., Norris, P., Ponarin, E., Puranen, B., et al. (Eds.). (2014). *World Values Survey: All Rounds – Country-Pooled Datafile Version*: www.worldvaluessurvey.org/WVSDocumentationWV7.jsp
   Madrid: JD Systems Institute.

7 Individualism-collectivism is a cultural value that distinguishes two different types of social interaction. Individualists put the self first in social encounters, collectivists put the group first. Hofstede, G. (2001). *Culture's consequences: Comparing values, behaviors, institutions and organizations across nations*. Sage. Individualism-collectivism is conceptually similar to the independent versus interdependent self. Markus, H.R., & Kitayama, S. (1991). Culture and the self: Implications for cognition, emotion, and motivation. *Psychological Review, 98*(2), 224. However, tightness-looseness is conceptually and empirically distinct from individualism-collectivism. See supplemental materials in Gelfand, M.J., Raver, J.L., Nishii, L., Leslie, L.M., Lun, J., Lim, B.C., ... Yamaguchi, S. (2011). Differences between tight and loose cultures: A 33-nation study. *Science, 332*(6033), 1100–4.

8 This story is not from one of our interviewees, but from an executive education student who shared it in one of Jeanne Brett's classes to help his classmates understand his experience in a tight culture. We used it here with his permission.

9 Brett, J.M., Gunia, B.C., & Teucher, B.M. (2017). Culture and negotiation strategy: A framework for future research. *Academy of Management Perspectives, 31*, 288–308.

10 The World Values Survey (WVS) is an international research program devoted to the scientific and academic study of social, political, economic, religious, and cultural values of people in the world. The project grew out of the European Values Study and was started in 1981 by its founder and first president (1981–2013), Professor Ronald Inglehart from the University of Michigan (USA), and his team. Since then, the WVS has been operating in more than 120 world societies. The project uses a comparative social survey, which is conducted globally every five years. The extensive geographic and thematic scope of the WVS, and the fact that the data are freely available to researchers around the world as are the findings of the core research team, has made the WVS into one of the most authoritative and widely used cross-national surveys in the social sciences. The WVS is the largest non-commercial cross-national empirical time-series

investigation of human beliefs and values. Available at www.worldvaluessurvey.org /WVSContents.jsp

11   The most recent WVS database (at time of writing) is Haerpfer, C., Inglehart, R., Moreno, A., Welzel, C., Kizilova, K, Diez-Medrano, J., et al., (2020). World values survey: Round seven-country –pooled datafile. Available at: www.worldvaluessurvey.org /WVSDocumentationWV7.jsp

12   A scatter plot comparing estimates of trust at the national level measured by the World Values Survey, the European Social Survey, and Afrobarometer Survey reveals a positive and very high correlation. Esteban Ortiz-Ospina and Max Roser (2016) - "Trust". *Published online at OurWorldInData.org.* Retrieved from https://ourworldindata.org /trust

13   www.worldvaluessurvey.org/WVSDocumentationWV7.jsp

14   There are both theoretical and empirical justifications for aggregating individuals' answers to questions about their culture to the national level. Theorists conceptualize norms as shared social perceptions. Cialdini, R.B., Reno, R.R., & Kallgren, C.A. (1990). A focus theory of normative conduct: Recycling the concept of norms to reduce littering in public places. *Journal of Personality and Social Psychology, 58*(6), 1015–26.

Research shows that social perceptions, also labeled descriptive norms, are theoretically more relevant and empirically more powerful than individual values or preferences when studying cross-cultural differences. Peterson, M.F., & Barreto, T.S. (2018). Interpreting societal culture value dimensions. *Journal of International Business Studies, 49*(9), 1190–1207; Shteynberg, G., Gelfand, M.J., & Kim, K. (2009). Peering into the "Magnum Mysterium" of culture: The explanatory power of descriptive norms. *Journal of Cross-Cultural Psychology, 40*(1), 46–69.

The reasoning underlying descriptive norms is that although there can be variability within cultures, people who experience similar environments, for example, with respect to history, geography, climate, and economic and political systems, come to share a common social interpretation of that environment. Empiricists test the validity of the theorists' reasoning regarding level of analysis statistically. The method used here to test the validity of aggregating to the regional level is the relative within-versus-between-region variance. If variability of national averages is greater within than between regions, we would not be justified in using regional differences. This was not the case with trust or tightness-looseness.

15   To standardize the national level data, we calculated the mean and standard deviation across the four regions we studied. We calculated a standardized score for each nation according to the formula "standard score equals the observed value minus the mean of the sample divided by the standard deviation of the sample."

16   We used analysis of variance to test regional differences in trust. The statistic $F(3, 42) = 23.09$, $p < .001$ was significant. Although ANOVA is used to test the difference between means of two or more groups, it does so by comparing the relative variation *around* those groups' means versus *between* those groups' means. The interpretation of the ANOVA results is that differences in trust between some regions were greater than the variance in trust within those regions.

17   The post hoc Bonferroni analysis shown in the table compares each region to each other region. LA = Latin America, EA = East Asia, ME/SA= Middle East/South Asia. The asterisk indicates a difference is statistically significant. For example, EA* in the second row indicates that EA is significantly different from LA. The fact that there is no asterisk next

to the ME/SA in row one of the table indicates that this comparison is not statistically significant.

Multiple Comparisons of Trust by Region

					95% Confidence Interval	
(I) Region		Mean Difference (I–J)	Std. Error	Sig.	Lower Bound	Upper Bound
LA	ME/SA	−0.20	0.25	1.00	−0.90	0.49
	EA*	1.54	0.32	0.00	−2.42	−0.66
	West*	−1.73	0.25	0.00	−2.42	−1.04
ME/SA	LA	0.20	0.25	1.00	−0.49	0.90
	EA*	−1.34	0.31	0.00	−2.20	−0.48
	West*	−1.52	0.24	0.00	−2.19	−0.86
EA	LA*	1.54	0.32	0.00	0.66	2.42
	ME/SA*	1.34	0.31	0.00	0.48	2.20
	West	−0.19	0.31	1.00	−1.05	0.67
West	LA*	1.73	0.25	0.00	1.04	2.42
	ME/SA*	1.52	0.24	0.00	0.86	2.19
	EA	0.19	0.31	1.00	−0.67	1.05

Dependent Variable: Trust

* The mean difference is significant at the 0.05 level.

18 Delhey, J., & Newton, K. (2005). Predicting cross-national levels of social trust: Global pattern or Nordic exceptionalism? *European Sociological Review, 21*(4), 311–27.

19 See the World Bank's ratings of nations on governance: https://info.worldbank.org /governance/wgi/

20 Correlations range from −1 through 0 to +1. A positive correlation implies that high scores on one index correspond to high scores on the other index. A negative correlation such as the one between trust and corruption indicates that when trust is high, corruption is low. The source of this correlation is www.worldvaluessurvey.org/AJPublications .jsp?CndPUTYPE=2&PUID=18&CndPUTYPE=2&PUID=18

21 Another negative correlate of trust is inequality. There is academic debate as to whether low trust causes corruption, corruption causes low trust, or both are caused by inequality. Eric M. Uslaner, who has studied this problem for many years, argues that trust, corruption, and inequality are caught up in a reciprocal spiral in which all three factors influence each other and are inextricably linked. Uslaner, E. (2013). Trust and corruption revisited: How and why trust and corruption shape each other. *Quality and Quantity, 47*, 3603–8. DOI: 10.1007/s11135-012-9742-z

22 Nobel laureate Herbert Simon introduced the idea of satisficing. See Simon, H.A. (1955). A behavioral model of choice. *Quarterly Journal of Economics, 69*, 99–118.

23 For a discussion of the benefits of trust, see Slemrod, J., & Katuščák, P. (2005). Do trust and trustworthiness pay off? *Journal of Human Resources, 40*, 621–46.

24 Tightness-looseness is measured as a descriptive norm. Please see endnote 14 for a thorough discussion of descriptive norms.

25 Extensive notes in the 2011 *Science* paper describe the psychometric properties of the
    tightness-looseness measure and report the statistical justification for aggregating to the
    nation level (Gelfand et al., 2011).
26 Gelfand et al., 2011.
27 A correlation is a statistical indicator of relationship between two or more things.
28 Gelfand et al., 2011.
29 The most recent source of tightness-looseness data is in the supplementary materials of
    Gelfand, M.J., Jackson, J.C., Pan, X., Nau, D., Pieper, D., Denison, E., ... Wang, M. (2021).
    The relationship between cultural tightness–looseness and COVID-19 cases and deaths:
    A global analysis. *The Lancet Planetary Health, 5*(3), e135–e144.
30 We used analysis of variance ANOVA to test regional differences in tightness-looseness.
    The statistic $F(3, 40) = 32.22$, $p < .001$ was significant. See endnote 16 for more informa-
    tion about ANOVA.
31 The post hoc Bonferroni analysis shown in the table compares each region to each other
    region. LA = Latin America, EA = East Asia, ME/SA= Middle East/South Asia. The *
    indicates a difference is statistically significant. For example, ME/SA* in the first row
    indicates that LA is significantly different from ME/SA. The fact that there is no asterisk
    next the West in row three of the table indicates that this comparison is not statistically
    significant. LA and the West are similarly loose.

Multiple Comparisons of Tightness by Region

(I) Region		Mean Difference (I-J)	Std. Error	Sig.	Interval Lower Bound	Upper Bound
LA	ME/SA*	−0.82	0.10	0.00	−1.09	−0.55
	EA*	−0.57	0.11	0.00	−0.89	−0.25
	West	−0.13	0.09	0.87	−0.38	0.11
ME/SA	LA*	0.82	0.10	0.00	0.55	1.09
	EA	0.25	0.11	0.19	−0.06	0.56
	West*	0.69	0.09	0.00	0.45	0.93
EA	LA*	0.57	0.11	0.00	0.25	0.89
	ME/SA	−0.25	0.11	0.19	−0.56	0.06
	West*	0.44	0.11	0.00	0.15	0.73
West	LA	0.13	0.09	0.87	−0.11	0.38
	ME/SA*	−0.69	0.09	0.00	−0.93	−0.45
	EA*	−0.44	0.11	0.00	−0.73	−0.15

Dependent Variable: Tightness-Looseness

* The mean difference is significant at the 0.05 level.

32 See Gelfand et al., 2021.
33 Gelfand, 2018. Michele Gelfand's book offers more information on the pros and cons of
    tight and loose cultures.
34 For example, whether people engage in self-enhancing behaviors or self-criticizing
    behaviors may depend on their cultural context. Kitayama, S., Markus, H.R., Matsumoto,
    H., & Norasakkunkit, V. (1997). Individual and collective process in the construction

of the self: Self-enhancement in the United States and self-criticism in Japan. *Journal of Personality and Social Psychology, 72,* 1245–67.

35 Gelfand et al., 2006.
36 Gelfand, 2018.
37 Gelfand et al., 2006.
38 Gelfand, 2018.
39 Although tightness is related to social homogeneity, the two concepts are different. Cultural heterogeneity-homogeneity refers to variability within the society of ethnicities, languages, religions, and tribal structures. Cultural tightness-looseness refers to the strength of norms, which are shared. Norm strength refers to the pervasiveness in a culture of shared perceptions about normative expectations and punishments. Research relating tightness to indices of societal homogeneity (Alesina, A., Devleeschauwer, A., Easterly, W., Kurlat, S., & Wacziarg, R. (2003). Factionalization. *Journal of Economic Growth, 8,* 194) shows a curvilinear relationship. Extremely socially homogeneous and extremely socially heterogeneous nations are tight compared to moderately socially heterogeneous nations. Gelfand, M J., Harrington, J.R., & Fernandez, J.R. (2017). Cultural tightness-looseness: Ecological affordances and implications for personality. In T. Church (Ed.), *The Praeger handbook of personality across cultures* (Vol. 3, Ch. 8). Santa Barbara, CA: Praeger.
40 Apart from highly diverse Singapore, most East Asian cultures are ethnically homogeneous.
41 Exhibit 2.5 treats cultural levels of trust and tightness-looseness as independent and orthogonal. This is justified theoretically and empirically. Theoretically, trust and tightness-looseness refer to different social processes. Trust refers to people's willingness to make themselves vulnerable to another; tightness-looseness refers to the strength of social norms and tolerance for deviation from those norms. Not surprisingly, elements of culture that co-vary with trust, such as the historical influence of Protestantism, good government, wealth, income equality, and low levels of corruption, are not the elements of culture that co-vary with tightness-looseness. Cultural tightness is associated with ecological threats from natural disasters and population density, and not from wealth or income inequality. Not surprisingly, the correlation at the national level of analysis for the 30 nations that have data in both exhibits 2.2 and 2.4 is $r = -.003$, $n = 30$. Recall from endnote 20 that a correlation varies between −1 and +1. A correlation as close to .00 as this one is not significant.

3. Middle East and South Asia

1 Halevy, N., Halali, E., & Zlatev, J.J. (2019). Brokerage and brokering: An integrative review and organizing framework for third-party influence. *Academy of Management Annals, 13,* 215–39.
2 See Bohnet, I., Greig, F., Herrmann, B., & Zeckhauser, R. (2008). Betrayal aversion: Evidence from Brazil, China, Oman, Switzerland, Turkey, and the United States. *American Economic Review, 98*(1), 294–310. These economists compared people, from the countries named in their papers' titles, playing the same economic risk games. They found that people were much less willing to take risks when the outcome was dependent on the trustworthiness of another person versus chance. They labeled this phenomenon *betrayal aversion* and discussed its significant economic impact. Interesting to us, they report that betrayal aversion was more pronounced in their Oman sample than in their other cultural samples.

3 Recall from chapter 2, particularly endnote 39, that tightness-looseness and homogeneity-heterogeneity are related but distinct concepts. Cultural heterogeneity refers to diversity in cultural attributes, such as ethnicity, language, tribe, and religion. Tightness-looseness refers to the strength of social norms and sanctions in societies. There is a curvilinear relationship between the two concepts of culture such that tight cultures are typically either extremely homogeneous or extremely heterogeneous. Gelfand, M J., Harrington, J.R., & Fernandez, J.R. (2017). Cultural tightness-looseness: Ecological affordances and implications for personality. In T. Church (Ed.), *The Praeger handbook of personality across cultures* (Vol. 3, Ch. 8). Santa Barbara, CA: Praeger.

4 Previous research on cultural tightness-looseness suggests that people from tight cultures often have an "adaptor" decision-making style as it relates to preferences for gathering and processing information, whereas people from loose cultures often have an "innovator" decision-making style. Gelfand, M.J., Nishii, L.H., & Raver, J.L. (2006). On the nature and importance of cultural tightness-looseness. *Journal of Applied Psychology, 91,* 1225–44.

4. Latin America

1 Erin Meyer concludes that trust in business is relationship-based in most nations of the world except the West. Meyer, E. (2014). *The culture map: Breaking through the invisible boundaries of global business* (p. 171). Public Affairs.

2 More information about factors that influence cultural tightness-looseness can be found in Michele Gelfand's articles published in *The Guardian*. Gelfand, M. (2018, September 17). Here's the science behind the Brexit vote and Trump's rise. *The Guardian*. Retrieved from: www.theguardian.com/commentisfree/2018/sep/17/science-behind-brexit-vote-trump; Gelfand, M. (2021, February 1). Why countries with "loose," rule-breaking cultures have been hit harder by COVID. *The Guardian*. Retrieved from: www.theguardian.com/world/commentisfree/2021/feb/01/loose-rule-breaking-culture-covid-deaths-societies-pandemic

5. East Asia

1 When communication is indirect, the meaning of the communication must be inferred from its context, what else was said, or, more importantly, what was not said. When communication is direct, the meaning of the communication can be inferred from the words in the message itself. It is not necessary to know the context of the communication to understand it. The seminal text describing this difference between high- and low-context communication cultures is Hall, E.T. (1976). *Beyond culture*. Garden City, NY: Anchor Press. Hall describes East Asian cultures as being high-context, indirect communication cultures whereas Western cultures are low-context, direct communication cultures. For more recent data supporting Hall's description of East-West differences in the structure of communications, see chapter 1 of Meyer, E. (2014). *The culture map: Breaking through the invisible boundaries of global business*. Public Affairs.

Relevant to the statement in the text that it is difficult for people from indirect communication cultures to give negative feedback, Meyer notes that people from cultures that communicate indirectly are more likely to use softer language (e.g., sort of, kind of) and understatements (e.g., we are not quite there yet) when delivering negative information (Meyer, 2014).

2 Hall, E.T. (1976). *Beyond culture*. Garden City, NY: Anchor Press.

3 An easy way to learn more about differences between direct and indirect communication is from the video at https://m-peck.wistia.com/medias/3jv738640j

The video tells the story of rattling bicycles and contrasts a direct versus indirect approach to addressing the problem.

4 Why a culture develops as high versus low context has not been the subject of much empirical research. Hall (1976) proposed what is basically an ecological theory. He suggested that population density affects the nature of language, and the nature of language manifests in communication. His reasoning is that when people live in dense proximity, they do not need an elaborate verbal or written language to communicate because they share context that allows them to communicate with few words. His example is a long-married couple. It seems unlikely that population density is the only underlying cause of the evolution of language.

6. The West

1 In situations where the risk of exploitation is great (e.g., negotiations), people who reciprocate information sharing become more cooperative and generate higher joint gains. Putnam, L.L., & Jones, T.S. (1982). Reciprocity in negotiations: An analysis of bargaining interaction. *Communication Monographs, 49,* 171–91; Weingart, L.R., Thompson, L.L., Bazerman, M.H., & Carroll, J.S. (1990). Tactical behavior and negotiation outcomes. *International Journal of Conflict Management, 1*(1), 7–31.

2 This quote comes from research conducted by Don Ferrin and colleagues, who report that trustworthiness perceptions and cooperation operate in a complex spiral in interpersonal and intergroup situations. Ferrin, D.L., Bligh, M.C., & Kohles, J.C. (2008). It takes two to tango: An interdependence analysis of the spiraling of perceived trustworthiness and cooperation in interpersonal and intergroup relationships. *Organizational Behavior and Human Decision Processes, 107,* 161–78.

3 Schmoozing can help people overcome interpersonal friction and facilitate cooperation during first encounters. Morris, M., Nadler, J., Kurtzberg, T., & Thompson, L. (2002). Schmooze or lose: Social friction and lubrication in e-mail negotiations. *Group Dynamics: Theory, Research, and Practice, 6,* 89–100.

4 People in loose compared to tight cultures are more likely to evaluate information or address problems by "thinking outside the box" rather than inside it. By implication, relying on the opinions of others is cautious, inside-the-box thinking. See page 46 of Gelfand, M. (2018). *Rule makers, rule breakers: Tight and loose cultures and the secret signals that direct our lives.* New York, NY: Scribner. See also Gelfand, M.J., Nishii, L.H., & Raver, J.L. (2006). On the nature and importance of cultural tightness-looseness. *Journal of Applied Psychology, 91,* 1225–44.

5 There are most definitely intra-regional differences in tightness. For example, in Northern Europe, Sweden is much tighter than its neighbor Finland and in the US, Southern states are much tighter than Northern states (Gelfand, 2018).

6 Western managers talked about professionalism. They preferred direct eye contact, a firm handshake, and signals of respect by wearing business attire but at the same time they tolerated when those social norms were ignored.

7 See Gelfand, 2018.

7. Similarities and Differences

1 Distefano, J.J., & Maznevski, M.L. (2000). Creating value with diverse teams in global management. *Organizational Dynamics, 29*(1), 45–63. These authors describe a set of skills that facilitate performance in multicultural teams. Their model is Map-Bridge-Integrate (MBI). Mapping, the first step, requires seeing team members' differences as cultural.

Bridging involves finding ways to link different cultural approaches together in ways that respect the nature of the original approach. Integrating implies making a new whole out of the sum of the parts.

2   Brett and colleagues have written rather extensively about coexistence leading to creativity in multicultural teams. The authors propose the norm of meaningful participation to facilitate involving team members from different cultures in the group's deliberations in Janssens, M., & Brett, J.M. (1997). Meaningful participation in transnational teams. *European Journal of Work and Organizational Psychology, 6,* 153–68. The authors further propose that allowing cultural differences to coexist will facilitate fusion teamwork and creativity in multicultural teams in Janssens, M. & Brett, J.M. (2006). Cultural intelligence in global teams: A fusion model of collaboration. *Group and Organizational Studies, 31,* 124–153. The authors test their predictions empirically on data from 246 members of 37 multicultural teams in Crotty, S., & Brett, J.M. (2012). Fusing creativity in multicultural teams. *Negotiation and Conflict Management Review, 5*(2), 210–34. Across teams, when team members were more highly culturally metacognitive, fusion teamwork and creativity were more likely. Cultural meta-cognition refers to an individual's level of conscious cultural awareness during cross-cultural interactions. It is a dimension of cultural intelligence. Ang, S., & Van Dyne, L. (2008). Conceptualization of cultural intelligence: Definition, distinctiveness, and nomological network. In S. Ang & L. Van Dyne (Eds.), *Handbook of cultural intelligence: Theory, measurement, and applications* (pp. 3–15). Armonk, NY: M.E. Sharpe.

3   Gelfand, M. (2018). *Rule makers, rule breakers: Tight and loose cultures and the secret signals that direct our lives.* New York, NY: Scribner.

4   Biculturalism implies behaving in ways consistent with the two cultural contexts, holding values consistent with each, and identifying with each. Biculturals use coping strategies from both cultures and can interact effectively with people from both societies. Chen, S.X., Benet-Martínez, V., & Bond, M.H. (2008). Bicultural identity, bilingualism, and psychological adjustment in multicultural societies: Immigration-based and globalization-based acculturation. *Journal of Personality, 76,* 803–38. Jenkins and colleagues report a fascinating study of foreign students becoming bicultural. They invited engineering students from East Asian and Western cultures in the fall of their first year in school to the psychology lab, put fMRI caps on their heads, and recorded their brain waves looking at pictures of objects in expected versus unexpected contexts. Western culture participants in their study did not pay much attention to the context, according to the patterns of their brain activity, but the East Asian participants did. By spring, East Asian participants' brain activity looked more like that of their Western classmates. Jenkins, L.J., Yang, Y.J., Goh, J., Hong, Y.Y., & Park, D.C. (2010). Cultural differences in the lateral occipital complex while viewing incongruent scenes. *Social Cognitive and Affective Neuroscience, 5*(2–3), 236–41.

5   Note that this similarity is not predicted by other cultural characteristics, such as individualism-collectivism. See endnote 7 in chapter 2. According to the individualism-collectivism framework, East Asia, a collectivistic culture, would be considered more relational than the United States, an individualistic culture. However, our research suggests the low-trust cultures of the Middle East/South Asia and Latin America place a stronger emphasis on building personal relationships than the high-trust cultures of East Asia and the West. Brett, J.M., & Mitchell, T.D. (2019). Searching for trustworthiness: Culture, trust, and negotiating new business relationships. *International Journal of Conflict Management, 31,* 17–39.

6   See the World Bank's ratings of nations on governance: https://info.worldbank.org/governance/wgi/

7   The exact quote is "So whatever you wish that men would do to you, do so to them; for this is the law and the prophets." *The Holy Bible Revised Standard Version,* 1953, Matthew 7:12.

8 Delhey, J., & Newton, K. (2005). Predicting cross-national levels of social trust: Global pattern or Nordic exceptionalism? *European Sociological Review, 21*(4), 311–27.
9 Exhibits 2.2 and 2.4 show that Latin American cultures are low trust and loose.

8. Searching for Trust during a Pandemic

1 The Chinese Spring Festival starts on the 23rd day of the 12th lunar month of the Chinese calendar and lasts for about 23 days, ending on the 15th day of the first lunar month in the following Chinese calendar year. In 2020, this festival began on January 25. See www .timeanddate.com/holidays/china/spring-festival
2 Travel within and into the East Asian region was restricted, requiring testing, willingness to quarantine, and, later in the ongoing pandemic, proof of vaccination.
3 We note that technology for online conferences quickly built platforms for informal "meet-ups."
4 Northwestern University's Institutional Review Board (IRB), which oversees social science research that involves human subjects, approved the methods used in the interviews before and after COVID-19. IRBs generally are concerned with the privacy of participants in social science research. The Northwestern IRB approved audio, but not video, recording of interviews for this project.
5 *Impact of the COVID-19 pandemic on trade and development: Transitioning to a new normal.* UN Conference on Trade and Development. United Nations Publication UNCTAD/OSG/ 2020/1. This report concludes that the impact of COVID-19 is asymmetric to the disadvantage of the most vulnerable people both within and across countries. https://unctad.org /system/files/official-document/osg2020d1_en.pdf

9. The Future of Searching for Trust

1 Please visit the following link for more information about the impact of COVID-19 on economic activity in East Asia. https://asia.nikkei.com/Opinion/China-s-economy-shines -as-post-COVID-recovery-gathers-pace
2 Pound, J. (2020). There's nearly $5 trillion parked in money markets as many investors are still afraid of stocks. CNBC. Retrieved from www.cnbc.com/2020/06/22/theres-nearly -5-trillion-parked-in-money-markets-as-many-investors-are-still-afraid-of-stocks.html Of course, not all the cash sitting in money markets is earmarked for new business development. People and corporations conserve cash for many reasons, including economic uncertainty, which was certainly true during 2020.
3 For more details about how cultural tightness-looseness affected behavior during COVID-19, see Gelfand, M.J., Jackson, J.C., Pan, X., Nau, D., Pieper, D., Denison, E., ... Wang, M. (2021). The relationship between cultural tightness–looseness and COVID-19 cases and deaths: A global analysis. *The Lancet Planetary Health, 5*(3), e135–e144.
4 For more information on the behavioral tendencies of people from loose cultures, see Gelfand, M. (2018). *Rule makers, rule breakers: Tight and loose cultures and the secret signals that direct our lives.* New York, NY: Scribner.

10. Points of Application

1 Hierarchy refers to the power dimension of Shalom Schwartz's structure of values. In hierarchical cultures, there is a clear social order, with some people in superior positions while others are in inferior positions. People in such cultures tend to accept their position

in the hierarchy and are expected to be modest and show self-control. In egalitarian cultures, everyone is considered to be equal, and everyone is expected to show concern for everyone else. Schwartz, S.H. (1992). *Universals in the content and structure of values: Theoretical advances and empirical tests in 20 countries.* San Diego: Academic Press.

2 Face, honor, and dignity are three different cultural logics of self-worth. Self-worth refers to people's sense of their value in society. In dignity cultures, self-worth is largely associated with an individual's sense of accomplishment – of goal achievement. In face cultures, self-worth is largely associated with the degree to which the individual fulfills social roles in accordance with social norms. In honor cultures, self-worth is largely associated with self-assessment of reputation, that is, what the individual thinks others think of the individual. Leung, A.K.Y., & Cohen, D. (2011). Within-and between-culture variation: Individual differences and the cultural logics of honor, face, and dignity cultures. *Journal of Personality and Social Psychology, 100*(3), 507. See Brett, J.M. (2014). *Negotiating globally.* Jossey Bass (pp. 28–39) for a discussion of the value of this cultural logic for negotiators. See Aslani, S., Ramirez-Marin, J., Brett, J., Yao, J., Semnani-Azad, Z., Zhang, Z. X., ... Adair, W. (2016). Dignity, face, and honor cultures: A study of negotiation strategy and outcomes in three cultures. *Journal of Organizational Behavior, 37*(8), 1178–1201 for an empirical study comparing negotiators from the three types of cultures.

3 Setting limits was not just relevant in the Middle East/South Asia region. It came up in one way or another in interviews in all regions. In addition to respecting personal limits, managers also appreciated when a partner would acknowledge limits about what the partner could and could not share in negotiation and what the partner's company could and could not do in terms of project timing, etc.

4 Aron, A., Melinat, E., Aron, E.N., Vallone, R., & Bator, R. (1997). The experimental generation of interpersonal closeness: A procedure and some preliminary findings. *Personality and Social Psychology Bulletin, 23,* 363–77.

5 Two guides may help you build cultural knowledge: Meyer, E. (2016). *The culture map (INTL ED): Decoding how people think, lead, and get things done across cultures.* Public Affairs; Morrison, T., & Conaway, W.A. (2006). *Kiss, bow, or shake hands: The bestselling guide to doing business in more than 60 countries.* Adams Media.

6 Earley and Ang offer the most widely used definition of cultural intelligence in their seminal book, Earley, P.C., & Ang, S. (2003). *Cultural intelligence: Individual interactions across cultures.*

7 Empirical evidence suggests there are four primary dimensions of CQ, including meta-cognitive, cognitive, motivational, and behavioral. Meta-cognitive CQ refers to an individual's level of conscious cultural awareness during cross-cultural interactions. Cognitive CQ refers to an individual's knowledge structures about cultural institutions. Motivational CQ refers to an individual's capability to direct attention and energy toward learning about and functioning in situations characterized by cultural differences. Behavioral CQ refers to an individual's capability to enact a wide repertoire of verbal and nonverbal actions when interacting with people from different cultures. Ang, S., & Van Dyne, L. (2008). Conceptualization of cultural intelligence: Definition, distinctiveness, and nomological network. In S. Ang & L. Van Dyne (Eds.), *Handbook of cultural intelligence: Theory, measurement, and applications* (pp. 3–15). Armonk, NY: M.E. Sharpe. For complete information about the empirical development of the measure, see Ang, S., Van Dyne, L., Koh, C.K.S., Ng, K.Y., Templer, K.J., Tay, C., & Chandresekar, N.A. (2007). Cultural intelligence: Its measurement and effects on cultural judgment and decision making, cultural adaptation, and task performance. *Management and Organization Review, 3,* 335–71.

8 Lynn Imai and Michele Gelfand suggest that people can improve their CQ by setting challenging and specific goals pertaining to cross-cultural adaptation.
   Imai, L., & Gelfand, M.J. (2010). The culturally intelligent negotiator: The impact of
   cultural intelligence (CQ) on negotiation sequences and outcomes. *Organizational
   Behavior and Human Decision Processes*, *112*(2), 83–98. For the effect of international
   assignments on CQ see Ng, K.Y., Van Dyne, L., & Ang, S. (2009). From experience to
   experiential learning: Cultural intelligence as a learning capability for global leader
   development. *Academy of Management Learning & Education*, *8*(4), 511–26. The Cultural
   Intelligence Center https://culturalq.com/ provides tools, training, and assessment to
   build CQ.
9 Gelfand, M. (n.d.) Mindset quiz: How tight or loose are you? Available at: www
   .michelegelfand.com/tl-quiz

Index

adherence to cultural norms, 6, 162n18; in East Asia, 65, 72–5, 78–9, 97–8; in Western culture, 89–90

behavioral flexibility, 90–1, 96, 98, 104, 154
biculturism, 171n4
Bolivia: statements from interviewees in, 54, 57, 58, 110, 111, 115, 119, 121, 123, 135, 142. *See also* Latin America
Brazil, 24–5, 56, 110–11, 164n6; statements from interviewees in, 1, 13, 19, 20, 53, 54, 56, 57, 58, 59, 110. *See also* Latin America
brokered introductions, 15, 17, 39, 41–2, 45–6, 49, 63, 66–8, 76–7, 79–80, 88, 102–3, 147; and due diligence, 87–9; and references, 114–15. *See also* brokering (key action)
brokering (key action), 12, 15–17, 102–3, 147; definition of, 17, 163n4; and due diligence, 87–9; in East Asia, 65–8, 70, 75–9, 102–3, 115, 123, 139–40, 147, 156; in Latin America, 54–5; in Middle East/South Asia, 39, 41–2, 45–6, 49, 102–3; and references, 114–15; in Western culture, 87–9

Chile: statements from interviewees in, 54, 57, 59, 101
China, 33, 66–7, 70, 76, 129–32; effect of and response to COVID-19 pandemic, 108, 116, 127, 130, 134, 137; statements from interviewees in, 1, 12, 13, 18, 19, 66–77, 108, 132, 137, 139. *See also* East Asia
Colombia: statements from interviewees in, 55, 57, 59
communication: direct, 72, 102, 148, 169n1 (ch. 5); indirect, 66–7, 70–2, 75, 78–9, 98, 102–3, 115, 147–8, 154–5, 169n1 (ch. 5); online, 113–19, 121–2, 124–5, 127, 135–7, 140–2
competence (CORR standard), 18, 94, 122–3, 139–40, 143, 145, 149–50; definition of, 19; in East Asia, 45, 65, 69–72, 74–5, 77–8, 94–5, 98–9, 103, 122–3, 148–50, 154–5; effect of COVID-19 pandemic on, 122–3; in Middle East/South Asia, 45–6
CORR (competence, openness, respect, rapport) standards, 2, 13, 18–20, 94, 96, 107, 139–40, 145 149–52; and cultural/regional differences, 20–1,